A GARDEN  STYLE BOOK

LITTLE POTTED GARDENS

[SIMPLE SECRETS FOR GLORIOUS GARDENS—INDOORS AND OUT]

MIMI LUEBBERMANN

PHOTOGRAPHS BY FAITH ECHTERME

CHRONICLE BOOKS

SAN FRANCISCO

D1416687

Library of Congress Cataloging-in-Publication Data:
Luebbermann, Mimi.
Little potted gardens: simple secrets for glorious
gardens, indoors and out/by Mimi Luebbermann:
photographs by Faith Echtermeyer.
            p.   cm.
"A Garden Style Book."
Includes bibliographical references (p. 106) and index.
ISBN 0-8118-1603-6 (pb)
1. Container gardening. 2. Plants, Potted. I. Title.
SB418.L84 1998
635.9'86—dc21   97-30800
                         CIP

Printed in Hong Kong

Cover and interior design by
Aufuldish & Warinner

Distributed in Canada by Raincoast Books,
8680 Cambie Street, Vancouver, B.C. V6P 6M9

10 9 8 7 6 5 4 3 2 1

Chronicle Books
85 Second Street
San Francisco, CA 94105

Web Site: www.chronbooks.com

Contents

POTS FOR A SUNNY WINDOWSILL   45

POTS FOR AN INSIDE GARDEN   53

POTTED BULBS   63

Introduction

Few people can live without plants. The genes of our ancestors who tilled the soil still urge us to grow things. The cadences of the life cycle—from the first tender spears of spring bulbs edging through just-thawed ground in the spring to the last leaves falling off the trees before winter's gray cold—are imprinted in our psyche, and unconsciously, we have a need to note their rhythm. Whether it is a few pots of cyclamen blooming in the center of the kitchen table or a rooftop garden of specimen plants, our hearts are eased by the presence of green growing things.

¶Of course, many of us live in cities hemmed in by concrete and asphalt, and most of the earth lies in the shade of high-rises or underneath parking structures. By using pots for growing, city gardeners can surround themselves with luxuriant plants on window ledges, fire escapes, rooftops, and counter tops. In fact, almost any plant can live contentedly in a container: Pots can hold trees, bulbs, shrubs, vines, annuals, and perennials. For those wishing to harvest crops for the kitchen, everything from herbs to lettuces to tomatoes and fruit trees thrives in pots. A small shady deck can raise crops of lettuce, chard, and leeks, while hanging containers of tomatoes or a tower of beans will flourish with a sunny exposure.

¶Not only city dwellers love pots. Gardeners with a patch of ground find potted plants a solution to many problems. If winter's chill threatens tender plants from tropical climates, then potted plants can simply be moved to a protected location. Pots of plants that bloom during rainy periods can be set under cover to keep the rain from bruising the blossoms or breaking the flower stalks. Potted gardens can grow where diseased soil, or soil as hard as pavement, has been a gardener's discouragement. Concrete may pave many garden areas, but pots cleverly arranged over the surface can become a labyrinth of green. Gardeners who have gophers that gobble up tender roots may turn to the protection of plants growing safely inside containers. Invasive plants neatly contained in pots can save a gardener hours of weeding work, as anyone who has had wily mint or runner bamboo escape into garden ground can attest.

¶Pots can also solve landscape design problems. Tall potted vines trained up a trellis introduce a vertical element into a garden bed. A lushly planted pot at the end of a path provides the focal point for a garden. A container of bamboo shields an outdoor space from passersby, or makes a green curtain to block off an urban view. Pots of night-blooming jasmine underneath a bedroom window bring garden perfume into a room. Tender plants dug into garden beds in their pots during warm weather can be lifted—pot and all—in the fall and moved inside.

¶Bulbs live contentedly in pots, providing a seasonal display of blooms from spring to fall. Forcing bulbs in pots, that is, starting them out in pots and bringing them inside to a warmer room to hurry the bloom along, gives you the joy of watching flowers burst forth in your living room. The fragrance of spring from paper whites, freesias, or amaryllis drifts through your home. When the blooms are spent, the pots can be returned outside to sit until the foliage dies down, when the bulbs can be lifted to store until the next year.

¶The newest trend in potted plants is to see them as sculpture, wedding the form of the plant to the shape and color of the container. Groups of pots simply planted with seeded grass and displayed on a glass table become living art objects. Cactus, so much like minimalist sculpture, can be placed to achieve a singular effect inside your home and out. A series of pots of barrel cactus along a walkway enlivens a plain environment with form and texture for surprising visual pleasure. Grasses shift gracefully in the wind and, planted in multiple containers, can provide a touch of whimsy. As much as we love the traditional soft look of a terra-cotta pot with a generous mixture of different plants, stylish monochromatic pots arranged as carefully as a still life makes a garden a creative accomplishment.

¶Gardeners have been using containers as long as they have been planting gardens. From the first (probably cracked) clay pots to old granite water troughs, to leaky coffeepots or even old sneakers, containers have always been dear to the hearts of garden zealots. A pot can be defined as anything that can contain a plant, from wire baskets to old birds' nests. Anything goes for pots, including flea market finds of willow laundry baskets, antique canisters, and old coal buckets splashed with paint to coordinate with the blooms of the plants contained within. Although most plants require pots that drain, water or bog plants will thrive in cachepots or urns, or any container that holds water. Regardless of the container, gardeners relish tucking all kinds of plants or even large fruit trees into pots so they can fuss over them and keep track of their every need.

¶The Victorians were enthusiasts for potted gardens, particularly within the house. Old housekeeping books show glass cases bursting with potted plants, windowsills slathered in ivies, and aspidistra poking up in all the dark corners. Every kind of forcing bulb imaginable transported bright garden colors into the often gloomy interior of the Victorian mansion. With the invention of industrial techniques to create sheets of glass, conservatories came into vogue, so exotic orchids and citrus just discovered by intrepid globetrotters could be grown in Europe year-round, despite the climate. The Victorians were, however, only a flowering of a custom whose roots are deep in history.

¶Along the banks of the Euphrates River in the sixth century B.C., King Nebuchadnezzar II decreed the building of the hanging gardens of Babylon for his queen. Terraces rose up into the sky filled with trees and vines, a grand example of the potted garden, which has been replicated throughout history in smaller roof gardens and in our own potted gardens on fire escapes and balconies. The Egyptian King Ramses III laid out hundreds of temple gardens with many potted shrubs on the west bank of the Nile, opposite Thebes. The Greeks set out containers to celebrate the Feast of Adonis, and both the Greeks and the Romans used terra-cotta pots in their gardens. The middle-class Romans of 100 B.C., who lived in buildings much like our apartment houses today, filled their stairways, balconies, and rooftops with potted plants.

¶The ancient tradition of rooftop gardening with pots sprouting alongside chimneys now makes good ecological sense by purifying city air while bringing gardening pleasure to city dwellers. Originally, roof gardens were a solution to riverside living, when annual floods swept away all crops and gardens. Modern inventions of waterproofing and steel for reinforcing roofs to bear the load of plants and soil have allowed even more extensive rooftop gardening. Le Corbusier and Frank Lloyd Wright are among the contemporary architects who designed rooftop gardens for private homes and public buildings. Should you want to continue in this tradition, be cautious of roof load, for a bevy of pots can represent a great deal of weight, more than some roofs can carry.

¶The ubiquitous terra-cotta pot, so essential to the gardener, has been shaped to humankind's use for hundreds and thousands of years. Assyrians, Persians, and Egyptians as well as the Chinese were using terra-cotta as early as 3000 B.C. The Mayans in Mexico were using terra-cotta by 2500 B.C. The famous Qin Dynasty soldiers, made from terra-cotta, date from about 221 B.C. The ancients sculpted and pressed clay into everything from water and plant containers to tiles and architectural ornaments, both glazed and unglazed, from inexpensive jugs to fantastically crafted reliefs, elegantly fashioned fountains, decorative medallions, and even church altars. The simple terra-cotta plant pots we buy in the gardening store today have not changed all that much from those used by our ancestors.

¶Although potting plants is an ancient art, the practice fits into our modern lifestyle perfectly. Whether you have limited ground space or limited time, potted plants can provide color, texture, blooms, fragrance, and fruits and vegetables year-round. Or you can simply indulge yourself by growing a dozen narcissus in a pot for snow-white blooms just when the melted snows outside turn black and dreary. A single orchid flashes out joyous blasts of color for months. A windowsill garden of herbs provides snippets of flavor for your meals. A lemon-scented geranium placed strategically in a passageway releases a fresh citrus fragrance whenever you brush by. Be wary though, for you may

discover that once you start collecting potted plants, they will take over your heart, home, and garden.

¶As a child, I entered miniature gardens in garden shows as a member of a Brownie troop in Central Elementary. In those days, tinfoil represented lakes and stream beds, but I am sorry to say that I can't remember any more of my designs than that they employed tiny plants and little rocks. My next memory of pot gardening is my dear godmother Emme's garden when I first visited her in spring. I was stunned to see pots and pots of tall daffodils, their bright yellow blooms swaying in the spring breeze. She showed me other pots of bulbs stored in her garage to bring out for months of spring bloom. Slabs of wood covered the pots to mimic winter dormancy. Emme first gave my children amaryllis to grow, and I will never forget their eagerness each morning to measure the bud's growth, and their total amazement as a bud unfurled into a glorious trumpet of bloom. Now almost one hundred years old, Emme continues her gardening tradition with ever-changing pots of blooms on a little glassed-in balcony.

¶When I started vegetable gardening, I turned to large containers to grow my winter lettuce. I found that two containers provided salad greens for my family throughout the mild California winter. By ringing the base of the containers with copper strips, I could discourage the voraciously hungry snails that chewed their way through the rest of my garden. This triumph led me to growing other vegetables in containers, covering my large concrete patio with sprawling vines of pumpkins and tomatoes planted in half barrels or large salad-bowl-shaped terra-cotta containers.

¶Despite these triumphs, my failures with house plants led me to despair. I tried the oh-so-easy spider plants and Boston ferns, even spathiphyllum and fish-tailed bamboo. As a new gardener, I didn't know how to take care of plants, and when the fern was down to its last frond and the spider plant died back, I had, with sorrow, to discard them. It took years of querying other gardeners and reading gardening columns and books before I learned to grow potted plants indoors by proper watering, fertilizing, and lighting.

¶After I moved to the country, I had the devastating experience of watching some forty tomato plants (tomatoes are one of my weaknesses) disappear into the ground, or simply fall over, their roots eaten off. The culprits were gophers, who were delighted that I had opened a cafe for them in my garden. All my attempts at trapping or eliminating them were foiled by my inexperience and their canny intelligence. As the days of early summer passed, with nary a tomato plant thriving, I realized that to have home-grown tomatoes at all, I would have to plant them in containers to foil the gophers' ceaseless feasting. Once again, containers provided a solution to my gardening needs.

¶Containers also protect all my plants that would otherwise freeze in winter's chilly night temperatures. A cactus collection that thrives outside on the deck in the warm summer days and temperate evenings comes inside over winter. My orchids, which enjoy the outdoor summer breezes, also come inside to be protected from chill temperatures that would otherwise almost instantly turn their leaves brown.

¶I have long experimented with displays of plants in coordinating containers, and when I am in garden supply stores, antique shops, or flea markets, I search out green glazed containers to add to my collection. Of course, I still use my old favorites, the standard terra-cotta, plain yet classic, a perfect foil for plants. Yet I have begun to play even with them by painting them in simple patterns of bold stripes.

¶Potted gardens never bore, but always challenge. I am dazzled by the boundless plant choices, ever intrigued by the quest for new containers, ever eager to grow new bulbs, to rearrange a clutch of pots. From a 1-inch pot bursting with emerald-green grass or the tiniest bulb lifting its miniature yolk-yellow head, to huge wood containers holding fruiting peach trees or a rainbow of summer geraniums bloom, the potted garden celebrates nature's riches. So revel in pots, arranging your containers, pouring in the mix, and setting in the plants to bring the whole green world to your doorstep for you to enjoy all year long.

CHARACTERISTICS OF POTTED PLANTS

Any plant can be grown in a pot, although the particular characteristics of each plant make it necessary to follow certain procedures to make them grow successfully. Understanding the characteristics of your plants helps you plan an existence for them that matches their requirements. Consequently, they will flourish, providing you with their best performance of flower, fruit, or foliage.

¶Plants are categorized as annuals, biennials, or perennials, indicating their life cycles. Annuals are quick-growing plants that grow, flower, set seed, and die in one season, such as zinnias, nasturtiums, or pumpkins. They range from the tiny Johnny jump-up to twining morning glories. Biennials grow to maturity and die back in two years, with growth in the first year and flowering and seed in the second. Perennials grow, flower, and produce seed for at least two years or much longer. Some perennials, including vines and small woody plants such as lavender, are especially well-mannered potted plants, but even large shrubs and small trees can be grown successfully in large boxes or containers. Perennials can be deciduous, losing their leaves in the fall, like roses and clematis, while others, such as rosemary and potato vines, are evergreens.

¶Bulbs bloom, then store up nutrients and plant matter for the next year. By the time they become dormant, all they need is next year's sun, warmth, and water to produce the bloom already curled up inside the bulb. Therefore, applying nutrients before bloom will not affect the flowers, but nourishing the bulb after bloom prepares it for the following year's glory.

¶Plants grow at different speeds. Some plants, like cactus, may seem hardly to grow at all from year to year, while a hop vine takes off in the spring and grows 30 to 45 feet by fall. These different growth rates mean that some plants outgrow their containers much quicker than others. The watchful gardener must judge when a plant needs to be moved into a new container.

¶Knowing the specific growth rate of your plant helps you judge the size of the container it needs to keep the roots growing vigorously. Some annuals, like pumpkins, grow explosively, with such gigantic green leaves and long running stems that they need a well-developed root system to provide enough food to fuel their growth. Tiny annuals like pansies stay miniature, and so are healthily maintained in smaller containers. Usually, the larger the mature plant, the larger the container it will require.

¶A too-small container with less space for root development than a plant needs may stunt the growth of a fast-growing plant so that it never fully develops, or its growth may be retarded. In the case of some plants, such stunting doesn't prevent its flowering or fruiting, although production will be limited compared with a plant grown in the ground.

¶Stunting is not always bad, and sometimes gardeners deliberately cause it in plants, as in bonsai gardening. Plants too large or invasive for a small garden can be held in check in pots. However, you must root prune regularly to keep the plant from becoming rootbound, meaning that the roots circle inside the container and become matted and inefficient.

¶Plants have different growing requirements based on their natural habitat. As natives, some plants grow on the forest floor. In your garden they want similar conditions, with filtered sunlight, a rich and well-fertilized potting mix, and a constantly moist environment. Put the same plant on a west-facing windowsill inside a dry house and it will literally fry to death. A desert cactus, accustomed to infrequent showers in its native habitat, will die if housed in a plastic container with a moisture-holding potting mix that is dutifully watered every week. Under these conditions, which are absolutely foreign to its normal habitat, its wet-sensitive roots will rot. A desert cactus needs a special cactus potting mix that allows the water to drain quickly. The formula of the mix, the type of container, and the site should all match the natural requirements of the plant.

¶Roots are the life blood of plants, but plants in pots are rather like goldfish in a bowl. A container is an unnatural environment for a plant, which the gardener needs to moderate. During the summer, in hot, westerly exposures, the blasting sun may heat the mix to triple-digit degrees. The roots—potted above the ground—are exposed to extreme temperatures as the sun beats down on all sides of the pot. Plants that like warm soil, such as summer vegetables and flowers, can benefit from heat, but take care that the plants stay well watered and temperatures inside the pot are not excessive. A vine such as clematis, which wants cool roots, suffers under such treatment.

¶In the winter, similarly, potted plants are overexposed to cold temperatures. The effects of wind chill and cold can gang up on a hardy plant, plunging the temperatures in the mix lower than your thermometer might indicate from the air temperature. The combination of being in a container and the effect of wind and cold may kill a plant that would easily survive if planted in the ground.

GROWING POTTED GARDENS

Unlike plants in the ground, with roots that wander far and wide in search of water and nutrients, plants in pots are captives. They must depend on you to provide the water and nutrition they would normally seek by themselves. If you understand how plants grow, you can better care for them, assuredly watering, feeding, and repotting them to keep them flourishing.

WATER

A plant is an efficient mechanism, with all its parts working to provide food and water for its growth and maturation. The roots are like straws drawing water and nutrients out of the soil into the plant. The water is sucked through the roots and drawn out onto the surface of the leaves, where the sun, warming the surface of the leaves, causes the water to evaporate through their pores. As the water evaporates, it pulls more water through the plant from the roots.

¶During periods of high evaporation from the leaves, such as hot or windy days, the rate of water loss increases, so the roots require more water. This process, called transpiration, explains why a healthy plant without water begins to wilt, and eventually can die from lack of water and nutrition.

¶When the leaves lose more water than the roots can quickly replenish, the plant wilts. Except for desert plants, a properly watered plant is one that has constant access to readily available water. Increase your watering when the weather turns hot or windy.

Small pots dry out faster than large ones, so check the water needs of little pots more often.

¶Just as plants can die from too little water, they can die from too much. In order to breathe, roots need oxygen, which they find in the spaces between soil particles. Normally, when an area of potting mix fills with water, gravity pulls the water down through the spaces between the particles, allowing oxygen to fill them again. But in a container, the lack of a drainage hole, a saucer filled with water so the mix cannot drain, or a layer of crockery at the bottom prevents proper drainage and can cause the roots to suffocate.

WATERING PRACTICES

The greatest challenge of container gardening is keeping pots sufficiently watered throughout the year. Because water so critically affects the life of a plant, particularly in a container, water your plants consistently. A drip system on an automatic timer with a separate mister attached to each container is an easy and effective means to keep container plants well watered.

¶Depending on how extensive a collection of pots you have, a simple, inexpensive system can be put together with parts bought from a hardware store. A manual system assembles quite easily, hooked up to a hose which you turn on daily or several times a week depending on the weather. There are more elaborate systems run by an electrical timer that water automatically, which are not difficult to install if electricity is handy.

¶A thin spaghetti tube runs off the main water line to each pot. Although you can somewhat disguise drip tubing by bringing it up the back of the container, if you add a tube up through the drainage hole when the pot is planted, it is almost invisible. The plant must be raised on bricks or blocks so the tubing is not crimped.

¶If you do not put your plants on a drip, make sure to water them regularly, checking at least 2 inches into the mix with your finger to make sure that the potting mix is thoroughly moist after watering, not just on the surface. You may need to drench the pot several times for better absorption or take further steps if the root ball has dehydrated (see page 39). If the weather becomes windy or hot—which increases the amount of water the plant uses—increase your watering and use a fine mister at least once a day on the leaves of the plants.

¶The time of day you water depends upon the weather and the plants. For those plants like squash and melon, with leaves susceptible to mildew, water early in the day so the leaves dry off by evening. If the weather is hot and dry, and your plants are not bothered by mildew, watering at night allows the water to sink into the mix before the temperature and sun dry it out.

POLYMERS/HYDROGELS

The latest technological advance in container gardening has come about with the introduction of polymers, sometimes called hydrogels, that are added when hydrated to the potting mix. When mixed with water, the dry beads swell up into tiny gelatinlike dots. As the mix dries, the roots penetrate the polymers to draw out the water. You can also hydrate polymers with a solution of fertilizer. After about 10 years, the polymers will biodegrade, but until then, they continue to respond to water, swelling up again and again when moisture comes in contact. Regardless of whether you have your pots on a drip system or water by hand, polymers, with their extra source of water, are useful in pulling plants through a patch of hot weather or inadequate watering.

¶The directions call for mixing either dry or hydrated polymers throughout the potting mix. However, gels have a way of working their way up through the mix to the surface. If you wish, add the planting mix and a layer of polymers to the bottom two thirds of the pot, adding pure mix to fill the pot up to the top. Read the directions carefully because if you use polymers hydrated with fertilizer, you will need to fertilize less often.

POTTING MIXES

Choosing the right mix for the type of plants you raise is essential to produce healthy root growth and, subsequently, healthy plants. Garden soil alone, scooped into pots without careful attention to amendments, may not drain well enough to keep your plants alive. Or, in some locations, it may drain too fast for many plants. In other locales, garden soil once potted into a container forms a hard soil block allowing for no water penetration at all. Untreated garden soil, brought inside, can also produce odors and harbor insects.

¶Not all commercial potting mixes are the same, for some are designed to drain quickly, and others to retain water longer. A sandy, fast-draining mix, such as one designed for cactus, allows water to flow through quickly, so the roots have less water available. A heavy mix with a high proportion of peat moss, by contrast, holds water in the mix and is preferable for plants like roses or sunflowers that prefer constantly moist soil.

¶In garden shops and nurseries, you will find both soil-based mixes and soil-less mixes. Soil-based mixes consist of sterilized soil along with amendments for texture. This soil has been sterilized to rid it of insect eggs, seeds, and soil-based fungi. Although you can sterilize soil in your own oven, you may find the odor of baking soil unpleasant. If you wish to try it, place 3 to 4 inches of soil in an ovenproof container. Moisten the soil thoroughly, and bake in a 200°F oven until an oven thermometer measures the temperature at 180°F in the center of the soil. Recipes for making your own potting mix (see page 101) use unsterilized garden soil. These mixes work best for outside pots.

¶Some commercial soil-based mixes also have fertilizer added to the mix. Adding more fertilizer to this kind of mix may harm your plants, resulting in burned roots and plant death. Seedlings are particularly root sensitive, and may not survive fertilizer overdose.

¶The soil-less mixes are made of peat moss mixed with sand, perlite, or vermiculite. Perlite and vermiculite are minerals heated until they puff up into small particles that provide the proper texture and composition to a mix. Soil-less mixes find favor with gardeners because plants consistently perform well in this kind of mix. They provide no nutrition to the plants, so adding fertilizers to aid in plant growth is essential.

¶Plant growth also depends on the chemistry of a mix and how well it meets a plant's needs. Although a majority of plants will grow in an almost neutral mix, some plants require an acid mix, others an alkaline. The pH (potential hydrogen) balance of a potting mix affects how well a plant absorbs nutrients. Acid plant mixes have a pH of 6.9 and lower; alkaline ones have a pH of 7.1 and higher.

¶Look for specialty mixes that have been formulated to meet the needs of plants with special requirements. There are mixes for azaleas and rhododendrons, cactus and orchids, ferns and roses. Check with your local nursery to find the potting mix that best meets the requirements of your plants, or tailor make your own (for recipes, see page 101).

FERTILIZERS AND NPK BALANCE

The major nutrients needed for plant growth are nitrogen, phosphorus, and potassium, usually identified by their chemical abbreviations N, P, and K. A plant in the ground takes these nutrients from the soil and uses them to grow stems, leaves, blossoms, and fruit or seeds. Containers planted with sterile potting mix, however, offer a plant no nutrition, for the mix is basically inert. Even containers with some soil or compost in their mix may not provide enough nutrition to feed a plant over its lifetime. Frequent watering, usually needed for container-grown plants, also leaches out nutrients. Adding fertilizer to the mix replaces missing or used-up nutrients. As an alternative or in addition, you can fertilize with a liquid fertilizer.

¶Studies have shown that potted plants grow better with doses of liquid fertilizer every 2 weeks, but many busy gardeners find that applying liquid fertilizer once a month is the best they can do. A monthly program, in conjunction with adding slow-release fertilizer granules to the potting mix when planting, seems a good compromise that brings satisfactory results. The slow-release fertilizers are

formulated in pellets designed to dissolve over time in the soil, depending on the temperature and the amount of moisture in the soil.

¶If you start a 2-week program, use an all-purpose liquid fertilizer diluted to half strength, as opposed to full strength for a once-a-month system. Make sure to follow the directions on the container for the correct dilution. Adding liquid fertilizer to dry soil can burn delicate feeder roots, the thin filaments on the outside of the root mass that absorb water and nutrition, so always water before you add liquid fertilizer.

¶Liquid fertilizers come with instructions for dilution, in proportions of water to fertilizer. Generally, these instructions are indicated for monthly applications. If you are fertilizing every 2 weeks, add twice as much water to make the dilution half strength.

¶Increase fertilizing during periods of rapid growth, when a plant's nutrient needs are greatest. Most plants spurt in spring and summer, although there are some exceptions to this rule, such as some types of orchids and cactus. Experts recommend decreasing fertilizing during fall and winter to allow the plant a period of natural dormancy, with no new tender growth that might be nipped by frost. If you have added slow-release fertilizer to the mix, you can stop fertilizing altogether with liquid fertilizer from November to about March, or until you see the plant begin to bloom or to grow again.

¶Commercial fertilizers list their contents as the percentage of each nutrient, in the order of nitrogen, phosphorus, and potassium. For example, an NPK formula of 10-10-10 has equal amounts of nitrogen, phosphorus, and potassium, while one of 20-20-20 is twice as strong. Some plants, such as tomatoes, need a formula with less nitrogen, which encourages leaf growth. When given too much nitrogen, tomatoes, like many other plants, will explode gloriously with leaves but with a minimum of flowers, resulting in large plants with almost no fruit. Potassium and phosphorous stimulate root and bloom growth. All-purpose fertilizers have a balanced formula for the maximum growth of roots, good leaf growth, and blooms. Although it may seem that if some fertilizer is good, more must be better, do not over fertilize plants. As with overfeeding people, too much fertilizer can encourage unhealthy excess growth.

¶You'll see on the shelves different fertil-

izers formulated specially for containers, from spikes, pencil-thickness stubs that poke into the mix, to granulated formulas that release slowly into the mix over several months. Spikes, although convenient, are less efficient, as their flow of nutrients is limited to the area of their placement, while adding a granulated slow-release formula throughout the potting mix assures better distribution to the roots.

¶Manufacturers' claims and scientific studies differ on just how long slow-release fertilizers continue to dissolve and release in the soil, for watering habits, temperature, and a plant's needs all produce different effects. For the best results, add slow-release fertilizer to the potting mix yearly and maintain a schedule of supplementing it with applications of liquid fertilizers.

¶Look for liquid fertilizers that are particularly formulated for containers. They include a variety of minerals and supplements important for potted plants. The old organic standby, fish emulsion, which used to be distinctly fish fragrant, has now been deodorized, so it can be used for plants indoors and out.

¶You may want to consider using organic fertilizers in your pots planted with edible plants. Although there have been no

conclusive studies, there are a number of testimonials to the improved taste of vegetables that are grown using organic fertilizers. Look for certified organic slow-release fertilizer granules to add to the mix before planting, and add liquid organic fertilizers diluted to half strength once or twice a month. Or you can add equal parts of blood meal (N), bonemeal (P), and wood ashes (K). Try different methods to find one that works best for you.

¶Bulbs contain all the nutrients they require for the current year's bloom. After bloom, however, they begin to store up food for the following year. Make sure to fertilize regularly after bloom to assure flowering performance for the next year. Never cut off a bulb's green leaves, for the leaves are essential to allow the bulb to process and store nutrients. When the leaves turn yellow, it is safe to cut them away. At that point, you can lift the bulbs out of the container and store them in a cool, dry place until you repot them, or if they do not crowd the container or are a type that likes to be crowded, you can simply leave them in the container. Store the container in a cool, dry place, but check periodically to make sure that snails or slugs didn't travel inside with the

container. You may find a bulb that is half eaten away or a snail trail, which looks like a translucent silvery ribbon. Snails and slugs can destroy bulbs by chewing into them whenever they get hungry. There is no need to water most bulbs while they are dormant. One notable exception is lily bulbs, which must be kept moist throughout the year.

CHLOROSIS

Occasionally, the newer leaves of potted plants begin to turn yellow between the veins, or in the case of conifers, the needles become an unnatural chartreuse color. Both are symptoms of a condition called chlorosis. If left untreated, the leaves will turn totally yellow and drop off. You can treat an affected plant with a special iron chelate formula that you add like liquid fertilizer to the potting mix, or you can spray the leaves with a foliar spray. If you suspect your plants have such a condition, take a number of leaves to your nursery for verification, as sometimes chlorosis can look similar to a viral disease. You need to know for sure what is wrong with your plant for effective treatment.

MULCHING CONTAINERS

Mulching your containers helps to retain moisture in the potting mix, particularly for plants set out in a westerly exposure. No matter how carefully you formulate your potting mix, if it is exposed to hot sun day after day, particularly in an unglazed terra-cotta pot, the mix will dry out, often hardening and shrinking away from the sides of the pot. When you water a dehydrated pot, the water simply rushes down the sides of the pot, never sinking into the root ball. A top layer of compost, spaghnum moss, or an inert material such as rocks helps to keep the sun's drying glare off the top of the potting mix, minimizing the sun's drying effect.

¶Not all plants need or like mulching, while some prefer one kind of mulch to another. Plants with naturally exposed roots, such as phalaenopsis orchids, do not grow well with mulches. Many types of orchid roots absorb nutrients from water and the air and, when kept constantly wet, rot quickly. Cactus and succulents like to dry out in between waterings, so a thick compost mulch does not match their growing needs. Compost mulches work best for those plants needing to be kept constantly moist, or pro-

tected from high temperatures because of their site's exposure. Make sure to pull the mulch back 1 inch from the stem to prevent keeping the stem too damp. Mulches also help to adjust the pH balance of potting mixes. If you are growing an acid-loving plant such as a camellia or rhododendron in a container, a mulch of bark or pine needles will decompose to add acidity to the mix.

¶A compost mulch, either purchased or homemade, blankets the tops of containers and adds nutrients to the potting mix as it breaks down. Because compost is constantly decomposing, however, you may not want to use it on house plants, as even subtle smells are noticeable indoors. For the most effective results, add compost to a depth of 2 to 3 inches on top of the mix. If you know when you plant that you wish to add a mulch, you can use a larger container and plant deeper, leaving more room at the top for the mulch.

¶Sphagnum moss acts as mulch while dressing up potted plants, particularly those you keep indoors. Its soft, frothy appearance hides the potting mix, which is quite useful for new plants that have not filled in. Like compost, it is not advised for use with plants that like to dry out between waterings or need their roots to stay exposed. Spaghnum moss loses its green color gradually, but exposure to sunlight speeds up this process.

¶Spanish moss provides a coarser mulch, and consequently, is less effective in preventing the escape of moisture. However, it adds a certain elegance and variety to a collection of indoor plants.

¶Rocks can be used to cover potting mix, contributing to the overall presentation, but with the added result of mulching. Black rocks in particular add an air of elegance. Rocks do, however, hold heat, so pair a rock mulch with a plant that needs the warmth, or use it to encourage a plant in the spring when extra warmth can add a boost to the plant's growth.

CONTAINERS

The shape of a pot affects the amount of room the roots have to grow. Square pots hold a larger volume of potting mix than cylindrical pots with sloping sides. The larger the volume of potting mix, the more room for roots to develop, resulting in a stronger, healthier plant. Some plants, such as daffodils, have long roots, so pots that are deeper than they are wide fit their growing needs. Plants with wide-spreading roots do better in shallow, broad planters. Other plants, such as amaryllis, need wide-based or heavy containers that will not topple over when they grow tall or top-heavy with bloom.

¶A large plant needs a large pot. The larger the plant, the more extensive its root system. Regularly check the drain hole of your containers to see if roots are beginning to show, indicating that the roots have begun to fill the container. For maximum continued growth of plants— especially vegetable plants, which need continued, rapid development in order to produce their harvest—repot when roots show at the bottom. For ornamentals like vigorously growing vines, not repotting can produce the desirable effect of minimizing growth. Stunted plants, such as bonsai trees, will continue to thrive indefinitely as long as you are vigilant and make sure they are well watered and fertilized regularly. Depending on the size of the plant and the container, you may need to root prune more than once a year in order to avoid a large plant in a smallish pot becoming root bound, which will inhibit its intake of water and nutrients.

TERRA-COTTA

The workhorse of containers is the terra-cotta pot. Made of inexpensive low-fired clay, these pots have been beloved by gardeners for thousands of years. Besides the simple least-expensive unglazed terra-cotta, glazed terra-cotta in shining colors adds beauty to the garden and can be chosen to coordinate with flower bloom. Unglazed pots must be watered more often because the clay breathes, and the pores allow moisture to escape and consequently potting mix to dry out quicker—perfect for plants that like to dry out in between waterings, but less suitable for moisture-loving plants. Unglazed terra-cotta pots are also more susceptible to cold weather, often cracking when they freeze. Glazing seals the pores of pots, letting the mix dry out more slowly and making the pot somewhat less susceptible to cracking.

¶If you like the look of unglazed terracotta but want the effect of glazed to preserve the moisture in the mix, consider applying a commercial terra-cotta sealer found in garden stores, or a masonry seal purchased at a tile, hardware, or paint store. Some imported unglazed terracotta pots have a greater tendency to crumble, particularly those shaped like

animals or with raised surfaces. Sealing these types prolongs their life. The sealer is simply applied inside and out of the pot with a paintbrush and dries clear with a matte finish, making the treated pots imperceptibly different from the unglazed pots. You can also choose to paint only the inside of the pot to diminish porosity while preserving the look of unglazed terra-cotta.

¶Older terra-cotta pots may acquire a coat of moss or a whitened look from leaching salts that some gardeners find desirable. This aged look can be achieved by painting pots with water-thinned yogurt and keeping them well watered and in a moist environment to encourage the growth of moss and fungi. For a different look, apply sphagnum moss with a glue gun.

OTHER TYPES OF CONTAINERS

¶Wood containers, from half wine barrels and old-fashioned asparagus grocery boxes to window boxes made from carved wood, make handsome containers for plants. Because the potting mix stays moist, wood can rot out quickly. Treat these containers with a nontoxic preservative, particularly important if you are growing edible plants. Barrels and half barrels need their hoops fastened in place by pounding small nails underneath the hoop, for should the barrel begin to dry out and shrink, the hoops often slip down. Check that the barrel has holes drilled in the bottom.

¶Plastic containers are eminently practical. Inexpensive and sturdy, they stack well for storage and do not react to freezing temperatures. Plastic retains water in the potting mix. Being lightweight, plastic containers are easier to move than terra-cotta or wood.

¶Although plastic is practical, it is less attractive than some of the other types of containers. Gardeners who use plastic often have wily tricks to obscure its pedestrian exterior. Using a plant surround (see page 84), a plant in a plastic pot can be slipped into a showy container. Elegant cachepots dress up plants in plastic pots for indoor display. Use sphagnum moss to cover the top of the container and obscure the rim.

¶Fiberglass containers often mimic large wooden boxes or terra-cotta pots but are so incredibly light, you can move the planted ones with an ease unknown with a wooden box of the same dimension. The handsome color is part of the fiberglass, so no upkeep is necessary.

¶Wire containers, from antique egg baskets to modern hanging vegetable baskets, make useful pots. Layer sphagnum moss next to the wire, then place nylon window screening on top of the moss to make an interior basket. The screening can be purchased at any hardware store and cuts easily with scissors. The moss showing between the wires makes a stylish presentation and the screening holds the potting mix. Pay these containers extra attention to make sure they don't dry out too quickly from hanging exposed in the air.

¶Sometimes you can find concrete containers that will take on the patina of an old horse trough quite quickly if treated with water-thinned yogurt. They are incredibly heavy, however, and need to be placed where you want them in the garden before potting them up with plants. The traditional planting of a trough is with tiny alpine plants, but they look fine planted with anything from daffodils to rhubarb.

¶Flea market finds can add whimsy and interest to a garden. Be creative, and a stylish motif can come from what others have labeled as junk. Old mailboxes, broken-down wheelbarrows, or even little red wagons can make a corner of the

garden a view destination. One creative gardener I know used an old truck, gorgeously painted with flames, as the container for an eruption of bougainvillea.

¶Metal containers, such as verdegris-stained copper or ultra-modern stainless steel, work well inside or out. Unusual or antique baking pans, gallon-sized European oil tins, old buckets, or metal watering troughs, as long as they have drainage holes, can become garden treasures. If you like, paint them with stripes, imitate spatter ware, or paint them to match your house for added interest.

SITE

Gardeners are often piqued to discover that a potted plant dwindles in one area while another similar plant thrives just a few feet away. Is it the individual plant, or are there other forces at work? Siting your containers to suit a plant's needs effects its successful growth. Some plants, such as varieties of ferns and hostas, like shade, while others, including many types of annual flowers and vegetables, want just about as much sun as they can get. In between the two comes filtered shade and filtered sun. But siting becomes more complicated when you add the factor of wind, or the plant's

exposure to morning sun versus afternoon sun.

¶Your garden is full of microclimates, some just feet away from each other. A sunny south-facing exposure is much different from a sunny west-facing exposure against a wall, which can produce reflected temperatures of over 100°F on only mildly warm days, baking a plant and its roots. If a plant doesn't grow well or looks lackluster in one spot, try it in another situation. If you have only a west-facing balcony, group plants together with the front pots shading those in back to help deflect wind and the sun's glare, tempering the burning heat.

¶Indoors on windowsills, the glare and heat right next to the glass is more intense than just inches back from the sill. Similarly, a windowsill site can chill sensitive plants as temperatures next to the glass plummet overnight. The morning light through an east-facing window is not nearly as hot or bright as that of a west-facing window. North windows provide light without direct sunlight. Just as you would with plants outside, experiment by moving plants around inside to find the light levels and temperatures that best approximate the plants' native conditions.

¶Never worry about bringing plants inside to enjoy their bloom period. This is one of the joys of a potted garden and not to be missed. The plant does not suffer from an interlude in a changed environment. To prolong the blossoms as long as possible, keep blooming plants in a cool room and out of direct sunlight, which can bleach the blooms.

LIGHT

Different plants require particular light levels, because in the wild they may grow under trees or out in a meadow in full sun. Certain sun-dwelling plants will become leggy and distorted if they have too much shade; like pining lovers, they reach for the sun. Shade-loving plants don't have the capacity to stand up to a full day's harsh sunlight, although they may tolerate some early morning sunlight, when the rays don't have their full potency. Most edible plants that produce leaves, fruit, or seeds need at least 4 to 6 hours of sun a day. Greens will accept a bit less direct sun, and if the pots are facing west and backed by a wall, the impact of warmth and reflected rays may make up for a shortened exposure.

¶When you place pots in a site, be aware of the light they receive. Don't forget that the light changes according to the season, for a pot that receives filtered light in spring may be exposed—to its detriment—to full sunshine in summer. The hottest exposure is against a west-facing wall, so plants in this site, unless they are desert plants or drought-resistant plants, need constant monitoring to make sure the potting soil doesn't dry out or the roots become too hot.

¶Drive a long-bladed knife down into the potting mix of a plant in a west-facing site in mid-afternoon. After 1 or 2 hours, pull out the knife and feel the blade. Depending on the size of the pot and the season, you may find the blade warm to the touch. This is an indication of the amount of heat the plant's roots experience. Over-heated roots dry out, needing even more moisture to protect the plant tissue and to work effectively drawing water out of the potting mix. This simple demonstration illustrates the rigors a potted plant may experience.

PLANT COMBINATIONS

Collections of plants living together in the same pot can either look dazzling or like an unmanageable thicket. When choosing plants to combine, consider the texture of the leaves as well as the overall

shape of the plant, and the colors of the leaves and flowers. For best results, limit yourself to three types of plants. One kind of plant should drape the container, another provide a vertical accent, and another fill in the spaces in between. Brightly colored flowers stand out against gray foliage, and variegated foliage looks elegant with white or cream-colored flowers. Plant different combinations and for your records, take a snapshot for comparison with other plantings.

¶You don't need to combine your plants in containers, for clustering single potted plants together can be quite dramatic, particularly if you only use one type of plant. If using different types of plants, try linking them together visually by keeping the pots in one or more shades of color. Vary the heights of the plants by setting the pots on risers of some sort or by using different sizes of pots, or even by setting a pot on top of its upside-down counterpart.

STARTING FROM SEEDS

Starting your own plants from seeds is easy, and it offers you the advantage of growing a wide range of varieties that nurseries do not regularly stock as baby seedlings or more mature starter plants. If you live in a cold climate with a short growing season, starting seeds inside produces vigorous plants that are ready for transplanting into outside pots when the weather warms up. Seeds also can be sown later in their permanent pots, when the warmth of spring encourages germination and there is no danger of frost. Whether you plan to sow indoors or outdoors, order your seeds for spring and summer sowing in January to make sure you start with fresh high-quality stock. (Some seed sources are listed on page 105.)

¶Check your nursery for seed-starting kits, such as Styrofoam flats, plastic six-packs, or peat pots. Choose pots or containers with individual sections for each seedling so that the transplants will pop out of them easily.

¶Seeds need temperatures from between 65° and 75°F to germinate. Some gardeners place heating mats specially designed to go underneath germinating trays to keep the soil evenly warm. A sunny south window may provide enough warmth and light. If not, hang fluorescent Gro-lights or full-spectrum lights 4 to 6 inches above the containers. If your plants lean toward the light source and look skinny and weak, they are not getting enough light.

¶Start your seeds 6 to 8 weeks before you want to put plants outside. Don't use soil

for sprouting seeds but instead use sterilized mix to avoid diseases that infect
seedlings. To make sure the plants get off
to a good start, add half the recommended
amount of an all-purpose slow-release fertilizer to the mix or, once the seedlings are
1 inch high, water them once a week with
a low-nitrogen fertilizer diluted to half
strength.

¶Thoroughly moisten the mix with
water, then fill the seed container to
within 1 inch of the rim. Check the recommended directions on the seed packet
and sow the seeds at the correct depth
and spacing. After you have sown the
seeds, sprinkle or sift mix over the top to
the depth specified on the seed packet.
Pat down the mix firmly and water carefully so you don't dislodge the seeds.
Keep the mix moist but not soggy to
avoid encouraging fungal infections.
Place the seed containers where they
will get 2 to 4 hours of bright sun a day.
If the seedlings begin to stretch up, lean
over, and look leggy, they are not receiv-
ing enough light. When the roots begin
to show at the bottom of the container,
the young plants are ready to be set out
of doors or into larger containers. Don't
let the plants become pot-bound, as this
can retard their growth.

HARDENING OFF SEEDLINGS AND YOUNG PLANTS

Because both seedlings and young plants
raised indoors or in a greenhouse are tender, you need to accustom them to the
more variable temperatures outdoors
before you set them into outside containers. This process is called "hardening off."
For 1 week before you plant them, set
them outdoors during the day only. Keep
them in the shade at first, then gradually
move them into the sun. When you plant
them, do it in the late afternoon, to lessen
the stress caused by the heat of the day.

VITAMIN B1

Although touted for years as the means to
lessen transplantation shock in plants,
studies of Vitamin B1 have shown that it
is ineffective in encouraging feeder
roots—the fine hairlike roots that absorb
nutrients for the plant—to regrow.
Although gardeners feel comforted by its
use, it does not speed plant recovery.
Keeping a transplanted plant well
watered and placing it in a shaded, wind-
protected area for several days while the
feeder roots regrow is the most effective
means of speeding a plant's recovery.

POTTING UP YOUR PLANTS

Many gardeners, to be on the safe side, scrub the inside of old pots with a chlorine solution as a precaution against soil-borne diseases. Gardeners who use soil-less potting mix, however, rarely scrub out their pots. Unless you know the pot has been inhabited by an infected plant, you can skip this step.

¶Almost every container-gardening book instructs the reader to add crockery to the bottom of a pot to improve drainage. This instruction uses up all those broken terra-cotta bits, but studies show that drainage is not improved, but **imperiled**. The layering of two different materials—the fine-grained potting mix on top and the crockery pieces on the bottom—can impede drainage. The mix drains perfectly well by itself. You can leave the hole at the bottom of the container uncovered if you wish, for after several waterings the mix will settle and not fall out. Or, you can cover the hole with a flat piece of crockery or square of nylon screening that retains the mix and prevents snails or slugs from hiding inside the hole.

¶To transplant, soak the plants in their pots or flats in a bucket or sink until they stop bubbling. If a plant is too large to fit into a bucket, water it thoroughly by

hose. Gauge the amount of potting mix you need to fill the new container and add slow-release fertilizer granules according to the directions on the container. Moisten the mix thoroughly. Add enough mix to the bottom of the new container to allow you to position the top of each root ball 1 inch below the rim of the container. If you choose to, add hydrogels at this time according to the directions.

¶Gently tap seedlings and small plants from their container, taking care to keep the root ball and its potting mix intact. Check the required spacing for the plants. Make sure to leave enough room so they do not become crowded as they mature. Make a hole in the container and set in the plants so the top of the root ball is level with the soil. Tamp down the soil firmly around the root ball, making sure the plant is set in securely. Water well. Keep the plants in the shade for 2 or 3 days, watering daily to lessen transplanting shock.

¶Turn larger plants on their side, or if size allows, upside down, and tug the plant gently to slide it out of the original container. If it sticks, tap the sides or bottom of the plant sharply. Root-bound plants may be harder to pull out; slide a knife around the sides to help free the plant.

Center the root ball in the pot and add moistened mix up around the sides. Tamp down the mix and water thoroughly. You may need to add more mix after you have watered to bring the level up to 1 inch below the rim of the container. Set the plant in a shaded, wind-protected area for several days while the feeder roots grow. Make sure to water daily. After 3 or 4 days, return the plant to its normal site. Continue to water daily for 1 week after potting.

REPOTTING

To keep potted plants healthy, repot them yearly. At this time, you can divide overgrown plants, trim the root ball to keep plants from becoming pot-bound, or simply move the plant into a larger pot to provide enough room for the next year's growth. The addition of fresh potting mix combined with slow-release fertilizer gives the plant a fresh start for the following year. When repotting, examine the roots. Few roots or roots that seem dried or rotten can indicate that you are damaging the roots either by using too much or too little water.

¶Plants that have overgrown their containers can be divided and the sections repotted separately. This is usually carried out after blooming, but always check the requirements of the specific plants because some plants, such as grape hyacinths, prefer to be tightly planted in their pots, while others do not want to be disturbed unless they are dormant. The best time to repot evergreen perennials is in the fall, after the yearly growth has finished. Repot deciduous plants in the winter, when dormant.

¶The overgrown roots of a pot-bound plant encircling the root ball must be trimmed back and spread out when repotting. Try to untangle the mass of roots, then cut the roots back so that when you repot, you can set them straight into the container without bunching or twisting them. The feeder roots, which grow from the tips of the main roots, will regrow quite quickly. Fast-growing plants like vegetables or vines can be put into a much larger container, while slow-growing plants like cactus need only the next size up. Add mix to the bottom and the sides of the container, positioning the top of the root ball 1 inch below the rim of the container. Pat the mix down firmly to make sure there are no air pockets and water thoroughly.

¶Plants in large containers that are too heavy to handle can be renewed yearly by top dressing. Dig out all the old potting mix you can in the container and measure the amount. Add an appropriate amount of slow-release fertilizer granules to new potting mix and add it to the container. Water the container well for the next 3 to 5 days, then return to the normal watering schedule.

CURING DEHYDRATED ROOT BALLS

When a root ball becomes dehydrated, the potting mix will become rock solid and shrink from the sides. The plant will droop and look faded and shriveled, with a white cast to its leaves. If the plant is small enough, totally submerge it, in its pot, in a bucket of water or a sink. Let it sit for at least 20 minutes, or until all the bubbling stops. Check the roots and repot the plant if they look overgrown and pot-bound.

¶For large plants that are too heavy to lift for submerging, cover the surface of the potting mix with ice cubes. The ice will melt slowly, allowing the water to penetrate the dry surface and to gradually be absorbed into the root ball. You may need to do this several times with a large plant, but once the surface has become absorbent, you can then water

in small amounts, letting the water sink in each time.

SUCCESSIVE PLANTINGS

Remember to plan ahead with your container gardening so you will always have several pots coming into bloom throughout the year. If your gardening time is limited, work on a pot-by-pot basis. Try to always have potting mix and some extra pots on hand so you can pick up a six-pack of blooming plants during your round of chores and pot them up for a quick burst of color. Even a windowsill meadow can chase away the winter blues and takes only minutes to create. The pleasure you receive is inordinate compared to the time spent on preparation.

TEMPORARY POTTED PLANTS

Don't forget that some plants work wonderfully as temporary indoor potted plants that you can enjoy for several weeks during a bloom period and then plant out in the ground. Flowering vines purchased in bud or bloom at a nursery can be slipped into a cachepot and enjoyed while blooming, then planted outside in the garden. Alternatively, many devoted plant admirers purchase orchids or other exotic plants that bloom only once a year and either send them to be boarded until the next bloom or donate them to the local botanical garden. Knowing their home doesn't match the plant's native conditions, they realistically assess that they will be unable to sustain the plants through the year.

¶Plants with burlapped root balls such as dogwood in bloom or small deciduous trees just leafing out can also be used as temporary house plants. Unwrap the burlap and encompass the root ball in plastic. Rewrap and fasten the burlap. Use the plant as a unusual centerpiece or table decoration for up to 2 weeks, watering weekly. Then transfer the plant to the garden, take off the plastic, restore the burlap, and plant.

FROST PROTECTION

Hardy and *tender* are two words tossed around by gardeners to roughly distinguish how well a plant withstands cold. Tender plants do not tolerate cold temperatures because water freezing in the plant tissue expands, damaging or destroying the plant. Hardy plants can stand up to a certain amount of cold and are often described as hardy to a certain temperature—for example, "hardy to 32°F." A third category, half-hardy plants,

will usually survive a cold spell, but may not survive extended cold weather.

¶One of the joys of gardening in pots is the ability to grow plants not suited to the winter temperatures of the garden. In cold climates like Minnesota, tropical plants can simply be carried inside to winter over, protected from the sub-zero temperatures outside. Depending on your climate, the south-facing wall of a house with an overhanging roof can provide protection and winter warmth for hardy plants. An attached garage or porch also shelter plants that can take some cold. Dormant plants need little light or water throughout the winter, but evergreen plants do. Check the individual requirements of your plants.

PESTS AND DISEASES

A variety of different pests may attack your plants, although well-watered and -nourished healthy plants appear to have an increased immunity. Try to identify the problem before you use any sprays or poisons, because insecticides only work for specific types of pests. Take the affected plant or leaves to your local nursery for identification. A number of insects, such as aphids or mites, can be washed off with a brisk spray of water, repeating as necessary. A mild infestation of scale can be scraped off with your fingernail or the back of a knife. Using potting mix avoids some pest problems, since the mix is free of the eggs or larvae often found in garden soil.

¶For edible plants, try the new series of organic soap-based pesticides that suffocate pests with fatty acids harmless to people and animals. For plants in an outside garden, research commercially available biological controls, such as lacewings and trichogramma wasps (very tiny and not like their larger annoying relatives), which attack plant pests without bothering humans. Consider using bacillus thuringiensis (BT), a bacteria spray that kills caterpillars without leaving any harmful residue. Although protecting your harvest by organic methods may be more labor-intensive, growing safe and nutritious food for yourself and your family is a clear incentive.

¶Slugs and snails can become persistent in the spring and fall and under moist conditions. One of the easiest ways to inhibit their entry into a container is to use copper tape to encircle the bottom of the container. When slugs or snails attempt to cross it, a chemical reaction produces a shock, stopping them from continuing. Buy the tape at hardware stores or garden shops. Alternatively, maintain a vigilant watch, going out in the evening with a flashlight to hand-pick slugs and snails into a bag containing several generous scoops of salt and discarding it, tightly tied, into the garbage.

¶Earwigs, those $1/2$-inch-long dark brown insects with the pincers at the end of their body, love to perforate tender leaves with dainty and not so dainty holes. Roll up a newspaper loosely and leave it next to the containers. In the morning, shake out the earwigs and step on them. It may take several nights for your earwig colony to move into the newspaper hotel, but persevere.

¶Viruses and fungi also attack plants, creating stunted and sometimes unusually colored plants. As soon as you notice any infected plants, discard them and their potting mix in the garbage. Do not reuse the potting mix, as it may carry the virus and infect other plants.

¶Whatever happens, don't become discouraged by failures. Some gardeners find indoor pots difficult because carefully cosseted greenhouse-raised plants—accustomed to an electrically maintained atmosphere and scientifically measured nutrition—don't always survive in the rough-and-tumble home environment. Finding the right site outdoors is equally tricky, for you will need to discover the right exposure. Determining the right plants for your house and garden is a question of trial and error. Soon, you will be able to judge whether a plant is flourishing in one area or needs to be shifted to another. The road to this knowledge is lined with the sad remains of potted plants, but take heart, all gardeners have had this experience.

¶Relish the obliging portability of your pots, lugging inside plants flushed with bloom, then banishing them outside again when flowering is done. Change your collections. Choose only gray plants one month, and the next, red-flowering types in hand-painted pots. Vary the heights, paint the pots to match or contrast with the blossoms, and experiment with combinations. Then, like an artist, survey your work, sighing with pleasure in your creativity and the deep satisfaction of caring for plants.

POTS FOR A SUNNY WINDOWSILL

Windowsill gardens—small gardens that just fit onto the narrow spaces of sills—might look easy, yet this location, so pleasing to the gardener, exposes plants to the hazards of living on the thin edge between indoors and out. Sunlight, intensified by the glare of the glass, can burn up a plant in a small container with little room for roots. In winter, an arctic chill seeps through the windows. Careful monitoring of conditions for the plants is essential for their success. When windowsill conditions are most extreme, moving the plant to a table or counter right next to the window may save its life. ❧ Indoors, light comes from one direction instead of totally surrounding a plant as it does outdoors. Consequently, plants will lean toward the light source, making it necessary to turn indoor pots regularly to keep plants growing upright. Light changes through the seasons as well, so the quality and quantity of light varies from month to month. A windowsill plant growing perfectly well in May can suffer from too little light in the same location in September due to the light shift. Monitoring the light paths in your home helps you care for your plants and also gives you a pleasant sense of the inclination of the earth and the change of the seasons. ❧ Even though windowsill gardens need special attention to their water and light needs, many different plants do well there, growing and blooming satisfactorily. Cactus are perfect windowsill plants, well suited to the climatic extremes of long-term windowsill tenancy—although winter cold must be watched. You can also feature plants on windowsills during their time of bloom, then switch them to other locations or summer them outside to keep them growing optimally. Repotting and root pruning will keep plants windowsill size.

A WINDOWSILL MEADOW

On gray and dreary winter days, we all need a reminder that spring can't be too far away. A friendly meadow can't help but cause a smile when you see it sitting cheerily on a windowsill. You can always star it as the centerpiece for a winter dinner, either alone or paired with forced spring bulbs. Quick to sprout and long lasting, winter wheat may not be as easy to find in nurseries but its wide leaf blades make a bold statement. Check feed stores or catalogues if your nursery doesn't stock it. Lawn seed with its finer leaf blades looks delicate and fragile and is equally appealing, particularly in small delicate pots that match its fine texture. Watch over your wheat lawn carefully, for some cats consider it a delicacy and may devour it. Should your meadow become a bit shaggy, a simple clipping with scissors gives a sheared effect.

¶ **HOW TO DO IT** ¶ Measure out the quantity of potting mix to almost fill the pot and add the correct amount of slow-release fertilizer granules according to the manufacturer's directions. Moisten the mix thoroughly, tossing to evenly distribute granules. Add mix to the pot to fill it 1 inch below the rim. Sprinkle the seeds thinly over the surface of the mix, cover with ¼ inch of potting mix, pat down, and water gently so you don't disturb the seeds. ¶ Place the pot in a sunny windowsill where it will receive 4 hours of sun daily. Water consistently to keep the mix moist but not soggy, and fertilize every 2 weeks with a soluble fertilizer diluted to half strength. If the meadow grows too high, snip it with scissors.

Winter Wheat, Annual Rye, Grass, Lawn Seed Mixtures
Triticum *species*, Lolium, *miscellaneous species*
❧

What You Need
Potting mix
All-purpose slow-release fertilizer granules
Containers, any size
Seeds
All-purpose liquid fertilizer
❧

Growing Conditions
3 to 4 hours of bright, sunny light
❧

Hardiness
Frost tolerant
❧

When Blooms Appear
In summer, if grass is left unclipped
❧

Cactus Collection

Many types of cactus flourish on windowsills, a site that mirrors their native desert habitat: burning hot sun during the day and low temperatures at night. Cactuses tolerate careless watering habits, although they, of course, must have some water to live. Remember the motto, "Better to underwater a cactus than to overwater it." Mammillaria, a widely available, beguilingly rotund cactus, will reside on a windowsill most of the year, with a mad fling of blooms for a period in spring or early summer. Buy cactus in bloom when you can, carefully checking that you have purchased the drought-loving desert cactuses. Windowsill conditions do not suit tropical cactuses, which require their potting mix to stay moist. ¶ **HOW TO DO IT** ¶ Place your cactus pots on a sunny east- or west-facing windowsill that receives at least 4 hours of sun daily. You may need to move them in winter to a south-facing windowsill. Water the pots less often in winter and, in the spring, begin to water more often, checking first to see if the potting mix has dried out. Water consistently, letting the mix dry out between waterings—the amount of time changes according to the temperature and the amount of sun the plants receive. Fertilize every month from April to October with a soluble fertilizer diluted to half strength. ¶ To repot, submerge the cactuses in their containers in a deep sink or bucket of water until the air ceases to bubble out. Use a page of newspaper folded into a thick long strip to hold each cactus while you slide it out of the pot. Toss cactus mix with half the correct amount of slow-release fertilizer granules specified in the manufacturer's directions. Add enough mix to bring the top of the root ball to 1 inch below the rim of the pot. Place each cactus in its new container and fill in the sides with mix, tamping it down. Water thoroughly. Do not fertilize newly repotted cactuses for 6 months.

Assorted Cactus
Mammillaria *species*

❧

What You Need
Mammillaria *cactuses*
All-purpose soluble fertilizer
Cactus potting mix
All-purpose slow-release fertilizer granules
*Container for repotting, one size larger
than previous container*

❧

Growing Conditions
4 hours of sun

❧

Hardiness
Tender

❧

When Blooms Appear
Spring to summer

❧

Miniature rose inside a rustic hoop

Miniature roses are all the rage, justifiably, for their tiny blooms can be exquisite, and their size makes them amiable to windowsill living. Often forced for availability at Valentine's Day, there are hundreds of varieties available in many different colors. Their standard plastic-pot residence makes them generic looking, but dressing them up makes them eligible for gifts. A change of pot helps, and creating a rustic hoop for the branches to grow through gives the plant a country air. Bare, still-green branches of shrubs or grapevines or fruit-tree trimmings are supple and can be bent to make hoops. If you need to, tie the branch ends with sisal or raffia. A hoop doesn't take many branches, so even city dwellers should be able to find enough material for this quick and simple project. Florist shops often discard trimmings that will work perfectly if no others are available. ¶ **HOW TO DO IT** ¶ When you bring your rose home, slip it into a cachepot or repot it into a handsome container. Bend a branch gently to make a rounded hoop and tuck the ends down into the potting mix or push them down the sides of a cachepot. Continue with the remaining branches, tying them with sisal or raffia. ¶ Place your rose on a sunny east- or west-facing windowsill that receives at least 2 hours of sun daily. You may need to move the pot in winter to a south-facing windowsill. Water consistently to keep the potting mix moist but not soggy, and fertilize every month with a soluble fertilizer diluted to half strength. ¶ To repot, submerge the plant in its container in a deep sink or bucket of water until the air ceases to bubble out of the container. Measure the quantity of potting mix needed to fill the new pot, taking into account the size of the plant's root ball, and add the correct amount of ❧

slow-release fertilizer granules according to the manufacturer's instructions. Add enough mix to the bottom of the container to bring the top of the root ball to 1 inch below the rim of the pot. Slide the rose out of its container and position the root ball in the middle of the new pot. Add mix around the sides, tamping it down as you go, and continue to add mix until it reaches the top of the root ball. Water thoroughly, and add more mix if the sides slump below the level of the root ball. ¶ Move the rose out of bright light to recover, watering it daily for 3 to 5 days, before replacing it on the sunny windowsill. Water consistently to keep the mix moist but not soggy, and fertilize once a month with a soluble fertilizer.

POTS FOR
AN INSIDE
GARDEN

C ompanion planting" means combining garden plants that benefit each other, but it could also describe growing plants inside our homes, where they almost become part of the family. Besides their friendly companionship, indoor plants are problem solvers. Cheerful greenery or blossoms can light up dark corners, focus attention in a room, or add a sense of drama to a long, featureless hallway. ❧ Be mindful of your plant's growing requirements, and duplicate them inside your home. Pick the right location based on the light levels available for the plant. In most homes, sunlight streams into east- and west-facing windows in summer, while during the winter, sun shines through south-facing windows. Sun-loving plants do well on windowsills or shelves with these exposures. ❧ A sensitive plant close to a

window, however, may receive too much sun, particularly in the afternoon. Should you see brown marks on the leaves, you will know the plants have been sunburned and should be moved back from the glass. You can also soften or mask the sunlight with a thin, gauzy curtain. Five or six feet back from a window, the light level drops dramatically, becoming as dark as twilight for a plant. Plants that live in dimly lit locations, such as forest-dwelling ferns or tropical jungle-floor plants, may be happiest with such a site or, alternatively, a location near a north-facing window, with bright light but no direct sunlight. If a plant doesn't thrive, try another windowsill or location that may suit it better. ❧ Plants inside a home generally receive light from only one direction, unlike the out-of-doors, where light surrounds the plant. Consequently, the light levels are diminished, and the plants will stretch toward the light, leaning awkwardly. Straighten the plant by turning it every few days. ❧ Be aware that watering pots can be hazardous to wood and other surfaces. Avoid unglazed terra-cotta saucers, using glazed or painted saucers underneath pots to avoid the moisture buildup that mars surfaces with white rings or stains.

SPRING FLOWERING BRANCHES

The magic of plant physiology allows a branch, even though cut from the tree, to follow its destiny by pushing out flowers and then small leaves. Even trees that don't flower in springtime perform the rite of spring, with leaves bursting forth from what was a tiny bump on a bare twig. ¶ If you have access, cut limbs from flowering shrubs or trees such as forsythia or flowering quince. Fruit trees such as almonds or plums are among the earliest to bloom in the spring, and prunings from them will produce delicately fragrant blossoms inside your house. So let the early spring storms rage, for you can walk into a room and inhale the fragrance from spring-flowering branches. ¶ **HOW TO DO IT** ¶ When the buds look swollen and show the first color, cut off the branches. Crush about 2 inches of the stems of the flowering branches with a hammer, or cut through the stems vertically with clippers to allow the stems to absorb water. Place the branches in a tall vase, adding stones to the bottom if the branches are long and threaten to overbalance the vase. Place the branches in a warm room to encourage the buds to open.

Branches of Flowering Trees
Forsythia
Forsythia *species*
Flowering Quince
Chaenomeles
Fruit Trees
Prunus
❧

What You Need
Flowering branches
Vase
Small stones (optional)
❧

Iron Cross Begonia

Discovered by plant explorers in the seventeenth and eighteenth centuries in tropical climates, begonias were named after the French botanist Michel Begon and were introduced to Europe in 1777. The family boasts a stunning variety of plants, some with showy, fragrant blossoms, and brilliantly colored, curiously textured, or curling leaves. Widely available at nurseries and florists, begonias provide indoor color and are easy to care for. ¶ A real showstopper, the iron cross begonia has leaves with an unusual and striking two-tone pattern of chocolate brown and green similar to a mason's iron. The flowers are inconsequential but the pebbly leaves grow 8 to 10 inches long. Place the iron cross in a sunny window location. Make sure not to overwater the plant, adding rocks to the saucer to lift the pot up above any moisture that might trickle out after watering. Let the potting mix dry out between waterings. ¶ **HOW TO DO IT** ¶ Place your begonia on a sunny east- or west-facing windowsill that receives at least 2 hours of sun daily. In winter, you may need to move the pot to a south-facing windowsill. Water consistently to keep the potting mix moist but not soggy, and fertilize every month with a soluble fertilizer diluted half-strength. ¶ To repot, submerge the plant in its container in a deep sink or bucket of water until the air ceases to bubble out. Measure the quantity of potting mix needed to fill the new pot, taking into account the size of the plant's root ball, and add the correct amount of slow-release fertilizer granules according to the manufacturer's instructions. Add enough mix to the bottom of the container to bring the top of the root ball to 1 inch below the rim of the pot. Slide the begonia out of its container and position it in the middle of the new pot. Add mix around the sides, tamping down as you go, continuing to add mix until it reaches the top of the root ball. Water thoroughly, and add more mix if the sides slump below the level of ↙

Iron Cross Begonia
Begonia masoniana
❧

What You Need
Iron cross begonia
All-purpose soluble fertilizer
Potting mix
All-purpose slow-release fertilizer granules
Container for repotting, 2 sizes larger
than previous container
❧

Growing Conditions
2 to 4 hours of sun
❧

Hardiness
Tender
❧

When Blooms Appear
Spring to summer
❧

the root ball. Move the plant out of bright light to recover, watering it daily for 3 to 5 days, before replacing it on the sunny windowsill. Water consistently to keep the potting mixture moist but not soggy, and fertilize once a month with a soluble fertilizer.

Elfin Forest

Tiny trees are showing up in nurseries and supermarkets more and more often. Miniature Christmas trees decorate the feast table, false cedars edge mantels, and Japanese maples handsomely decorate a terrace. A windowsill filled with little trees makes a display, or you can plant them all in one container as a miniature forest. Hang a basket of these on a door instead of a wreath, during the holiday season or any time of year. ¶ Little trees need bright light to grow, so if you exhibit them temporarily in a dim-light situation, return them to a sunny position soon thereafter. These plants have long-growing tap roots, so plant them in deep pots and check their root growth every several months during the summer. If you want to keep them quite small, you must root prune them at least twice a year—once when you repot and once in the middle of the summer. If you wish, you can shape and prune the trees to look like bonsai. Make sure to keep the potting mix moist, for little trees can dry out quickly. They appreciate being summered outdoors.

¶ **HOW TO DO IT** ¶ Place your trees on a sunny east- or west-facing windowsill that receives at least 2 hours of sun daily. In winter, you may need to move the pots to a south-facing windowsill. Water consistently to keep the potting mix moist but not soggy, and fertilize once a month with a soluble fertilizer diluted to half strength. ¶ To repot, submerge the trees in their container in a deep sink or bucket of water until the air ceases to bubble out of the container. Measure the quantity of potting mix needed to fill the new pot, taking into account the size of the plant's root ball, and add the correct amount of slow-release fertilizer granules according to the manufacturer's directions. Add enough mix to the bottom of the container to bring the top of the root ball to 1 inch below the rim of the pot. Slide the trees out of their container. Check to see if the roots have started to wrap around the root ball. With a pair of sharp clippers, ✒

Tiny Trees
Assorted varieties
❧

What You Need
*3 small conifers or Japanese maples
in 3-inch pots
All-purpose soluble fertilizer
Potting mix
All-purpose slow-release fertilizer granules
3 containers for repotting, each 2 sizes
larger than previous container*
❧

Growing Conditions
2 to 4 hours of sun
❧

Hardiness
Hardy
❧

cut off any encircling roots. Position the root balls in the middle of the new pot. Add mix around the sides, tamping down as you go, continuing to add mix until it reaches the top of the root balls. Water thoroughly, and add more mix if the sides slump below the level of any root ball. ¶ Move the plants out of bright light to recover, watering daily for 3 to 5 days, before replacing them on the sunny windowsill. Water consistently to keep the potting mix moist but not soggy, and fertilize once a month with a soluble fertilizer.

Ivy topiary

Gardeners have taken their shears to plants since the earliest gardens: Bringing plants to a protected place and arranging them in a certain order was only the beginning of shaping both space and plants to make a garden pleasance. Hedges have been shaped and cut into human and animal forms, curving or geometrical mazes and labyrinths, and long allées leading to a view site since the first Roman topiarius, a landscape gardener who practiced topiary. According to the Oxford Book of Gardens, Pliny the Elder wrote about the fantastic topiaries in Roman gardens, cut into forms as extravagant as hunting tableaux or shipping fleets. ¶ You need not go that far. Ivy makes one of the best topiaries, for you can keep plants inside or move them outside without damage. There are many varieties of ivy, from variegated ferny leaves to more common broad-leaved types. Easy to care for and forgiving of neglect, ivy topiaries make a visual statement alone or combined with other pots. ¶ **HOW TO DO IT** ¶ Place your topiary on a windowsill with sun or bright light. Water consistently to keep the potting mix moist but not soggy, and fertilize every month with a soluble fertilizer diluted to half strength. ¶ To repot, submerge the transplant and its container in a deep sink or bucket of water until the air ceases to bubble out. Measure the quantity of potting mix needed to fill the new pot, taking into account the size of the plant's root ball, and add the correct amount of slow-release fertilizer granules according to the manufacturer's directions. Add enough mix to the bottom of the container to bring the top of the root ball 1 inch below the rim of the pot. Slide the ivy out of its container and position it in the middle of the new pot. Add mix around the sides, tamping down as you go, continuing to add mix until it reaches the top of the root ball. Water thoroughly, and add more mix if the sides slump below the level of the ✒

Ivy
Hedera *species*
❧

What You Need
Ivy topiary
All-purpose soluble fertilizer
Potting mix
All-purpose slow-release fertilizer granules
*Container for repotting, 2 sizes larger
than previous container*
❧

Growing Conditions
Sunny or bright windowsill
❧

Hardiness
Depends on variety
❧

root ball. Move the plant out of bright light to recover, watering daily for 3 to 5 days, before replacing it on the sunny windowsill. Water consistently to keep the potting mix moist but not soggy, and fertilize once a month with a soluble fertilizer.

POTTED
BULBS

The joyful, splashy colors of bulbs titillate even the most jaded gardener. Although pots of daffodils, hyacinths, and spring crocus may seem to be the highlight of the bulb year, don't neglect bulbs that

bloom the rest of the year. Look for spring-blooming bulbs at nurseries in autumn, but check back in early spring for summer-blooming bulbs like tuberous begonias, lilies, and tuberoses. Autumn crocus and colchicums stretch the season into fall, and narcissus and amaryllis can be water-forced to bring bloom inside in winter. ❧ Planting spring or summer bulbs in pots allows you to move them under shelter if hard rains or hail threaten the blooms. Winter bulbs can be potted up for indoor blooms weeks before they occur outside. Pots, just coming into flower, can be brought to an entryway or terrace to spotlight them in full-blooming glory. If you bring blossoming pots inside, keep them in a cool room and out of direct sunlight to prolong the bloom. ❧ Always buy the best-quality bulbs you can afford. Try to buy daffodils or narcissus with double bulbs that produce two blooms per bulb. Shop at the beginning of the season for the best selection, picking out bulbs that feel firm when you squeeze them and have no signs of any damage or mold. Buy the largest bulbs in the bin. ❧ If you missed out on buying bulbs, you don't have to forfeit the season. Nurseries and florists sell pots of bulbs just ready to bloom. Bring them home and slip them into one of your own favorite pots, or load several small pots into a larger cachepot and cover with sphagnum moss. You can even decant the bulbs out of their pot, gently wash off the roots, and display them in water like water-forced bulbs. ❧ Although it's tempting to tidy up bulbs after they have bloomed, make sure you do not cut off their leaves until they have turned yellow. The leaves help the plant produce and store nutrients for bloom the following year. If you cut off the leaves while they are the least bit green, you will damage the bulb. Store the plants out of sight but in a sunny location and continue to water them regularly. To assure a healthy bulb and flowers for the next year, fertilize every 2 weeks after bloom with an all-purpose liquid fertilizer diluted to half strength.

AMARYLLIS

Like Theocritus and Virgil, Ovid, writing at the beginning of the first millennium, wrote pastorals, love stories about simple shepherds and their sweetheart shepherdesses, many of whom were called Amaryllis. Two thousand years later, we grow the amaryllis in our homes, but why the fat bulb should be named after a love-soaked shepherdess remains a mystery. Perhaps the rapid rise of the stem, which pokes out of the bulb and ascends so quickly you can almost see it grow, was reminiscent of the emergence of love. Perhaps the three or four large blooms that tower a good 12 to 16 inches up on the stem looked like trumpets announcing love's reign along the meadows. We may never know, but you will grow to adore the generous, heart-renderingly beautiful flowers that break the fast of winter and promise the feast of spring to come. ¶ **HOW TO DO IT** ¶ In the late fall, pot up your amaryllis bulb. Measure the quantity of potting mix to almost fill the pot and add the correct amount of slow-release fertilizer granules according to the manufacturer's instructions. Moisten the mix thoroughly, tossing to evenly distribute the granules. Add mix to the pot to fill it half full, and position the bulb root end down so that one third of the top is above the rim of the container. Add more mix below the bulb if necessary to raise it, and add mix around the sides, tamping down as you go. Continue to add mix until it reaches to 1 inch from the top of the rim. Water again thoroughly, and add more mix if the level drops. ¶ Place the plant inside in a sunny location. As the stem grows, rotate the pot to keep it growing straight. Use a stake to support the flower-heavy stem. Water consistently to keep the potting mix moist but not soggy, and fertilize every 2 weeks after ✣

Dutch Amaryllis
Amaryllis hippeastrum
❧
What You Need
Amaryllis bulb
Potting mix
All-purpose slow-release fertilizer granules
Container, 9 inches wide
by 9 inches deep
All-purpose soluble fertilizer
❧
Growing Conditions
Sunny windowsill
❧
Hardiness
Tender
❧
When Blooms Appear
Early winter to spring
❧

bloom with an all-purpose soluble fertilizer diluted to half strength. When the
foliage dies down in late summer, stop
watering and fertilizing and let the bulb
go dormant. Lift the bulb from the pot,
or store the bulb, still in the pot, in a
cool, dark place. In winter, when you are
ready to start again, repot as above,
bring the pot out into the light, and start
regular watering.

WINDOWSILL HYACINTHS

In Greek legend, Hyacinth was a beautiful young man loved by Apollo. Zephyrus, the jealous god of the west wind, caused a discus thrown by Apollo to kill poor Hyacinth, and the flower that sprang up from his blood was named after him. Despite this violent origin myth, the hyacinth merits a starring role on your windowsill for both fragrance and bloom. Hyacinths enjoyed a flare of popularity in the eighteenth century, with the Dutch propagating over two thousand varieties. Now, we are limited to a handful of types in colors of blue, white, and pink. ¶ So when winter becomes dreary and cold day after day, remind yourself that spring is really not so far away by water-forcing hyacinths on a windowsill. The leaves will unfurl to reveal a single stem like a candle, bearing row after row of trumpetlike small flowers, each one opening slowly. Forcing a plant this way exhausts the bulb, so it may take it several years to bloom again when planted in the ground, if ever. It's probably best to throw the bulb in the compost when it has finished blooming. ¶ **HOW TO DO IT** ¶ Use a container with a small enough neck to prop the bulb up with the bottom barely touching the water. Glass jars, glass pitchers, or traditional bulb-forcing cups allow you to see the roots grow, but any container that will hold the bulbs above the water works. Place the containers in a cool, dark place for 2 to 3 months, depending on the temperature. Check periodically and add water as necessary to keep the bottom of the bulbs barely touching water. ¶ When 3 or 4 inches of root fill the containers and the stems are 3 inches tall, bring the containers out of the darkness. Let the plants sit in dim light for several days. Gradually move the plants into brighter light and a warmer room. Once the foliage is deep green, the plants can sit on a sunny windowsill. When the buds begin to open, take them out of the direct sun to prolong your display.

Dutch Hyacinth
Hyacinthus orientalis

What You Need
5 bulbs
5 narrow-necked glass jars,
pitchers, or forcing vases

Growing Conditions
Cool, dark place during root development;
sunny windowsill for bloom

Hardiness
Hardy

When Blooms Appear
Early winter to spring

DOUBLE-PLANTED DAFFODILS

Daffodils grow in clusters, adding a new attached bulb every year. These additional bulbs, called noses, each produce a bloom. To produce a showy effect, plant two levels in a large pot for an extravagant display worthy of celebrating the return of spring. The spearlike leaves of the bottom layer will easily dodge the thicket of roots from the bulbs above. Three or four double-planted pots will resemble, as Wordsworth put it, "a host of golden daffodils." ¶ **HOW TO DO IT** ¶ In the late fall, pot up your daffodil bulbs. Measure the quantity of potting mix to almost fill the pot and add the correct amount of slow-release fertilizer granules according to the manufacturer's instructions. Moisten the mix thoroughly, tossing it to evenly distribute the granules. Add mix to the pot to fill it by one third and position half the bulbs root-end down, spacing them close together but not touching. Add another third of the mix, and place the rest of the daffodils as before, but with a bit more space between them. Continue to add mix until it reaches to 1 inch from the top of the rim, tamping down as you go. Water again thoroughly, and add more mix if the level drops. ¶ Keep the pot in a cool dark place for at least 3 months, watering only once every 3 weeks. After the last frost, bring the pots out into bright shade, then, as the foliage greens, into sunlight. Water consistently to keep the mix moist not soggy, and fertilize every 2 weeks after bloom with an all-purpose soluble fertilizer diluted to half strength. When the foliage dies down in summer and turns completely yellow, stop watering and fertilizing and let the bulbs go dormant. Lift the bulbs from the pot, or store the bulbs, still in the pot, in a cool, dark place. In fall, when you are ready to start again, repot.

Daffodils
Narcissus *species*
❧

What You Need
Potting mix
All-purpose slow-release fertilizer granules
Container, 16 inches wide
and 12 inches deep
24 daffodil bulbs, medium to tall variety
All-purpose soluble fertilizer
❧

Growing Conditions
Cool, dark place during root development;
sunny outdoor site for bloom
❧

Hardiness
Hardy
❧

When Blooms Appear
Early to late spring
❧

A SPRING GARDEN FOR MOTHER'S DAY

With a bit of preplanning, you can create a glorious potted display of tulips and forget-me-nots for an unforgettable Mother's Day gift. Plant up the tulips in the fall, over-wintering them carefully in a cool, dark place until 2 months before Mother's Day—about March 1. Bring them out into a warm, sunny location and water thoroughly. Plant forget-me-nots around the edge. If the weather is cold and the growth seems too slow to produce flowers by Mother's Day, bring the pot inside to a sunny location in a warm room. If growth is too fast, find a cool place to locate the plant outside. ¶ **HOW TO DO IT** ¶ In the second week of December, pot up your tulip bulbs. Measure the quantity of potting mix to almost fill the pot and add the correct amount of slow-release fertilizer granules according to the manufacturer's instructions. Moisten the mix thoroughly, tossing it to evenly distribute the granules. Add mix to the pot to fill it by one third and position half the bulbs root-end down, spacing them close together but not touching. Add another third of the mix and place the rest of the tulips as above, but with a bit more space between them. Continue to add mix until it reaches to 1 inch from the top of the rim, tamping down as you go. Water again thoroughly, and add more mix if the level drops. ¶ Keep the pot in a cool dark place for at least 4 months, watering only once every 3 weeks. Bring the pots out into bright shade, then as the foliage greens, into sunlight. Bring the pot indoors when the buds are well formed but not yet showing color. Water consistently to keep the potting moist but not soggy, and fertilize every 2 weeks after bloom with an all-purpose soluble fertilizer diluted to half strength. When the foliage turns totally yellow and withers in summer, stop watering and fertilizing and let the bulbs go dormant. Lift the bulbs from the pot or store them, still in the pot, in a cool, dark place. In fall, when you are ready to start again, repot.

Tulip
Tulipa, *any late-season variety*
such as 'Angelique'
Forget-Me-Nots
Myosotis alpestris

❧

What You Need
Potting mix
All-purpose slow-release fertilizer granules
Containers, 17 inches wide
and 14 inches deep
24 tulip bulbs
6-pack of forget-me-nots
All-purpose soluble fertilizer

❧

Growing Conditions
Cool, dark place during root development;
sunny outdoor site for bloom

❧

Hardiness
Hardy

❧

When Blooms Appear
Late spring

❧

Rembrandt tulips

The tulip, a seemingly artless spring flower, has in its history enough skullduggery, outright thievery, pirate smuggling, and histrionics to merit a place in a textbook on the rise and fall of empires. From the oft-mentioned seventeenth-century tulipomania to today's smuggling of species types from their native wild places, tulips, with their silky petals and limber stems, have inspired both greed and reverence. ¶ In the twentieth century, plant breeders discovered that introducing a virus to the bulbs created blooms streaked with white. They used a late-blooming variety known as Darwin tulips, named after Charles Darwin. These plants, despite their fabulous blooms, had the drawback of spreading disease; consequently the original Rembrandts were outlawed. Now the new types come from cross-breeding, their streaky blooms disease-free. Also known as Darwin tulips, these late-blooming beauties will crown your May breakfast table with any of several colors.

¶ **HOW TO DO IT** ¶ In the late fall, pot up your tulip bulbs. Measure the quantity of potting mix to almost fill the pot and add the appropriate amount of slow-release fertilizer granules according to the manufacturer's instructions. Moisten the mix thoroughly, tossing it to evenly distribute the granules. Add mix to the pot to fill it by one third and position half of the bulbs root-end down, spacing them close together but not touching. Add another third of the mix and place the rest of the tulips as above, but with a bit more space between them. Continue to add mix until it reaches to 1 inch from the top of the rim, tamping down as you go. Water again thoroughly, and add more mix if the level drops. ¶ Keep the pot in a cool, dark place for at least 4 months, watering only once every 3 weeks. Bring the pots out into bright shade, then as the ✈

Rembrandt Tulips
Tulipa 'Rembrandt'

❧

What You Need
Potting mix
All-purpose slow-release fertilizer granules
Container, 16 inches wide
and 12 inches deep
16 tulip bulbs
All-purpose soluble fertilizer

❧

Growing Conditions
Cool, dark place during root development;
sunny outdoor site for bloom

❧

Hardiness
Hardy

❧

When Blooms Appear
Late spring

❧

foliage greens, into sunlight. Water consistently to keep the potting mix moist but not soggy, and fertilize every 2 weeks after bloom with an all-purpose soluble fertilizer diluted to half strength. Bring the pot indoors when the buds are well formed but not yet showing color. When the foliage dies down in summer, stop watering and fertilizing and let the bulbs go dormant. Lift the bulbs from the pot or store them, still in the pot, in a cool, dark place. In fall, when you are ready to start again, repot.

POTS FOR A TERRACE GARDEN

The word terrace has a grand ring to it, but in truth, the definition of a terrace can include any outdoor platform, from a condominium balcony to a fire escape, a roof garden carved out between venting pipes, or a handkerchief-sized back deck on a city apartment building. Even the dingiest of localities filled with pots of bulbs, vines, and perennials becomes a true garden, with verdant growth punctuated by color and fragrance. ❧ Nurture pots to the point of bloom on terraces, and when the buds begin to color, carry them indoors for the full pleasure of the blossoms. When the bloom has finished, take them back outdoors. Fragrant flowers in pots can be moved underneath a living room or bedroom window so the sweet perfume drifts through. ❧ The terrace garden can also act as a framed work of art. Calculate the location of your pots for the enhancement of your view from inside your house. If you have a chair inside by a window, arrange the plants outside, then seat yourself to judge the view, shifting the pots around until you create a pleasing picture. ❧ In a larger garden, a collection of pots can become a destination and, alongside a garden bench, a place to pause momentarily. Canny gardeners with a strong color sensibility design their plant collections to harmonize in bloom color and to make an overall statement with subtly contrasting textures. The flashy fall colors of some shrubs, for example, make an exciting backdrop for a collection of potted plants. ❧ Make sure to enjoy your pots, not letting yourself grow bored by using the same old plants. Switch arrangements, vary the heights of pots, try new locations and new combinations, and pot up plants in fanciful or hand-painted creations.

Pluming grasses

T hanks to the heightened ecological awareness of gardeners today, grasses—many of which were once thought of as weeds—have come into their own as important garden plants. One of the most numerous and useful of plant species, providing food for both humankind and animals, grasses suddenly have been elevated from their long-recognized pragmatic status to that of a graceful orna- mental. And when you consider the sway of bamboo, the fall colors of Miscanthus, and the varieties of fescue, admiration becomes unbounded. Because many grasses are drought tolerant, they are particularly suited to pot culture. For a stylish dis- play, set out only one variety of grass in multiple containers. Plume grass, with its fine texture and whim- sical look, is a good choice, although you may find that once you start growing it, you will begin collecting other grasses. Alternatively, use a single grass plant among a variety of different plants in a container for a vertical accent. ¶ **HOW TO DO IT** ¶ Plant your pots after the last chance of frost has passed. Before planting, submerge the plants in their containers in a deep sink or bucket of water until the air ceases to bubble out of the containers. Measure the quantity of potting mix to almost fill the pots and add the correct amount of slow- release fertilizer granules according to the manufacturer's directions. Moisten the mix thoroughly, tossing it to evenly distribute the granules. Add mix to the pots to fill them to 2 inches below the rim. ¶ Scoop out enough mix to make a planting hole for each plant. Slide each plant out of its container and position the root ball in the middle of the planting hole. Add mix around the sides, tamping down as you go, continuing to add mix until it reaches the top of each root ball. Water again thoroughly, and add ✍

more mix if the sides slump below the level of the root balls. ¶ Place the containers outdoors in a shady place for the plants to recover, watering them daily for 3 to 5 days, before placing them in their permanent site. Water consistently to keep the potting mix moist but not soggy, and fertilize monthly with a soluble fertilizer diluted to half strength.

SPRING ICELAND POPPIES

The Iceland poppy originally came from Arctic regions, but the hot, vibrant tints of its crinkly flower petals belie its icy ancestry, and although many gardeners grow them as annuals, they are hardy perennials. They are easy to raise from seed, but Iceland poppies are widely available as starts from nurseries. Grown in pots, they can be hurried under cover if spring rains threaten to dash apart the flowers or winds to tear away the petals. In mild-winter areas, they can be started at Thanksgiving for early spring bloom. This is one plant that looks elegant planted singly in smaller pots because of its graceful flower stems. The 12- to 14-inch-tall flowers lift their heads high from stems bare of leaves, the reason for the Latin name, nudicaule. Of course, you can gang them in a large pot for a knock-out display of color. ¶ Iceland poppies make excellent cut flowers, the flowers lasting almost a week, and even after the petals are gone the pods make an elegant statement. Cut the flowers with a knife the first thing in the morning, then seal the cut stem in a candle or match flame. To keep them blooming in their pots, cut off the flowers after the petals start to fall but before they make seed pods. Dry the stems with the immature pods upside down to use in dried arrangements.

¶ **HOW TO DO IT** ¶ After the last chance of frost in the spring, pot up your plants. Before planting, submerge the plants in their containers in a deep sink or bucket of water until the air ceases to bubble out of the containers. Measure the quantity of potting mix to almost fill the pot and add the correct amount of slow-release fertilizer granules according to manufacturer's instructions. Moisten the mix thoroughly, tossing it to evenly distribute the granules. Add mix to the pot to fill it to 2 inches below the rim. Scoop out enough mix to make a planting hole for each plant. Slide each plant ✦

Iceland Poppy
Papaver nudicaule
❧
What You Need
6-pack of Iceland poppies
Potting mix
All-purpose slow-release fertilizer granules
6 containers, each 6 1/2 inches wide
by 6 1/2 inches deep, or 1 container,
12 inches wide by 12 inches deep
All-purpose soluble fertilizer
❧
Growing Conditions
4 to 6 hours of sun
❧
Hardiness
Frost tolerant
❧
When Blooms Appear
Spring or late fall
❧

out of its container and position the root ball in the middle of a planting hole. Add mix around the sides, tamping down as you go, continuing to add mix until it reaches the top of each root ball. Water again thoroughly, and add more mix if the sides slump below the level of any of the root balls. ¶ Place the container outdoors in a shady place to allow the plants to recover, watering daily for 3 to 5 days, before placing it in its permanent site. Water consistently to keep the potting mix moist but not soggy, and fertilize once a month with a soluble fertilizer.

LITTLE WATER GARDENS

Not everyone has the space or plumbing for a reflecting pool dotted with water lilies, much less a pond with white swans serenely gliding over the surface. Yet anyone can make a water garden elegantly topped with a blooming lily, even in a pot only 2 feet wide. Water gardens beckon to thirsty birds and insects. Even on the smallest garden, the wind will riffle across the surface. Place your pot in an area where you often sit so you can enjoy it at your leisure, or make sure you can see thirsty birds fly in for a sip as you sit in your favorite chair inside your house. The one hazard is overplanting your water garden. Like too many different flowers in an arrangement, too many different types of water plants in a small container can look haphazard. Try starting off with just water lilies. ¶ Water lilies come in hardy and tropical types, the hardy ones being a bit easier to grow. Like many garden plants, some water plants grow quite large, but others satisfactorily contain themselves, so regardless of the size of your pot, you can find plants appropriate to it. Miniature water lilies fit the scale of a smaller container. Be sure to include some fish, whether small, inexpensive goldfish or mosquito fish, to eat mosquito larvae. If you live in an area with raccoons, you may need to surround the pot with wire or plastic netting to keep the critters from dining on your succulent plants and fish. ¶ **HOW TO DO IT** ¶ Buy water lilies already started in plastic pots. Fill your water garden up to the top with water. Add the water lilies in their containers, placing the top of the containers holding standard-sized water lilies 8 to 12 inches under the water, and containers of the miniature types 4 to 6 inches under the water. Use cement blocks or bricks to elevate the containers to the proper level. Add slow-release fertilizer granules to the water each spring according to the manufacturer's instructions. When adding fish, let them become accustomed to the temperature of the water first by floating them in their plastic bag or container in the pot. Release them directly into the pot after 2 to 3 hours.

Water Lily
Nymphaea *species*
❧

What You Need
Water lily plants
Container without a hole, such as a half wine barrel or large ceramic pot at least 24 inches wide by 20 inches deep
All-purpose slow-release fertilizer granules
❧

Growing Conditions
2 to 4 hours of sun each day
❧

Hardiness
Some hardy, some tender
❧

When Blooms Appear
Summer to fall
❧

SUNFLOWERS IN POTS

Old-fashioned sunflowers can tower 10 to 12 feet tall, their monstrous round heads following the path of the sun through the summer sky. Yet don't think that you must pass up sunflowers because they are too large for pots. Smaller hybrid types now abound in petaled raiment from old-fashioned butter yellow to shades of cream, orange, deep maroon, and even halos of two-toned colors. The centers can be chocolatety brown or almost black, or with unusual fluffy or furry textures. Seed catalogues usually give the heights for different types, so choose low-growing ones for pot culture. Some of the multi-branched types produce excellent cut flowers. ¶ If you wish, you can also grow edible-seed sunflowers in large pots; however, they won't grow as large or produce as colossal a flower head as they do in the ground. Make sure to stake them carefully, for they cannot develop the root structure in pots to support their height and the weight of their heads, and a strong breeze may tip them out of their pots. ¶ **HOW TO DO IT** ¶ Plant your sunflower seeds after the last chance of frost has passed. Soak the seeds in water for 12 to 24 hours before planting. Measure the amount of potting mix to almost fill the containers and add the correct amount of slow-release fertilizer granules according to the manufacturer's instructions. Moisten the mix thoroughly, tossing it to evenly distribute the granules. Add mix to the pots to fill them to 2 inches below the rim. Plant 6 seeds in each pot. With your finger or a pencil, make a hole 1 inch deep. Drop in the seed, cover it with mix, and tamp the mix down. When all the seeds are planted, water gently to avoid displacing the seeds. ¶ Place the pots outdoors where they will receive 4 to 6 hours of sun daily. Water consistently to keep the potting mix moist but not soggy, and fertilize every 2 weeks with a soluble fertilizer diluted to half strength.

Sunflowers, Italian White,
'Sunbeam', 'Valentine',
'Chianti', 'Sunset'
Helianthus species

❧

What You Need
18 seeds
Potting mix
All-purpose slow-release fertilizer granules
3 containers, each 24 inches wide
by 20 inches deep
All-purpose soluble fertilizer

❧

Growing Conditions
4 to 6 hours of sun each day

❧

Hardiness
Tender; sow for summer only

❧

When Blooms Appear
Summer

❧

PLANT RING

Clever gardeners who love potted gardens have a kind of a cheat pot, which miraculously always looks like a permanently planted container. Actually, this pot is the result of a gardener's sleight of hand. A ring of permanent plants encircles an empty plastic pot sunk into the center of a large, impressive planter. The empty pot allows you to slip in a container of annuals, perennials, or even a small shrub during its peak bloom. As the blooms begin to fade, you whisk away the container of spent plants, to be replaced with a new container. The assemblage of a planting ring and a plant bursting with seasonal blossoms looks gorgeous. For maximum impact, place this pot in an area of high traffic volume, and you will be assured an appreciative audience for your ingenuity. ¶ One of the most endearing surround plants is lamb's ears, with its drooping gray fuzzy leaves, but variegated ivy also works well to add a drape around the planter as a contrast to vertical-growing plants. ¶ **HOW TO DO IT** ¶ Plant your pot after the last chance of frost has passed. Place the large container in its permanent position, as it will be heavy to move. Before planting, submerge the plants in their containers in a deep sink or bucket of water until the air ceases to bubble out of the containers. Measure the quantity of potting mix to almost fill the pot and add the correct amount of slow-release fertilizer granules according to the manufacturer's instructions. Moisten the mix thoroughly, tossing to evenly distribute the granules. Add mix to the pot to fill it to 4 inches below the rim. In the center, push out the mix to make room for the plastic pot that will hold the container of seasonal blooms. ¶ Position the plastic pot in the center hole, with its top at the level of the mix. Add enough mix to the large pot to fill it 2 inches below the rim, leaving the center pot empty. Then, in the mix in the large pot, scoop out enough mix to make a planting hole for each plant of ✦

Lamb's Ears
Stachys byzantina
❧

What You Need
Container, 19 inches wide by
15 inches deep
Two 6-packs of lamb's ears
Potting mix
All-purpose slow-release fertilizer granules
Plastic container, 9 inches wide
by 9 inches deep
All-purpose soluble fertilizer
A seasonal plant in a 9-inch container
❧

Growing Conditions
4 to 6 hours of sun
❧

Hardiness
Tender; protect from winter cold
❧

When Blooms Appear
All year long, depending on
what is in bloom
❧

the surround. Slide each plant out of its container and position the root ball in the middle of a planting hole. Add mix around the sides, tamping down as you go, continuing to add mix until it reaches the top of the root balls. Water again thoroughly, and add more mix if the sides slump below the level of any of the root balls. ¶ Water consistently to keep the potting mix moist but not soggy, and fertilize once a month with a soluble fertilizer diluted to half strength. Protect the plant surround over winter, as lamb's ears is not frost-hardy. ¶ For the center of the ring, choose a plant in bloom in a 9-inch pot that takes sun. Slip the container into the plastic container. When blooms begin to fade, switch the container with another plant in bloom.

POT OF WILDFLOWERS

When we think of native wildflowers, images of prairies and long vistas carpeted with great patches of blooming color come to mind. Lacking the wide-open spaces of the country, you don't need to forswear the joys of wildflowers. Local nurseries or wildflower catalogues sell mixtures of seeds. Sown thinly in the early spring directly into a large container, the plants will erupt in a season of mad flowering. Let the flowers go to seed, gather up the dried seed heads, and save the seeds for your pots the next year. ¶ **HOW TO DO IT** ¶ Plant your wildflower seeds after the last chance of frost has passed. Measure the quantity of potting mix to almost fill the pot and add the correct amount of slow-release fertilizer granules according to the manufacturer's instructions. Moisten the mix thoroughly, tossing it to evenly distribute the granules. Add mix to 1 inch below the rim. Sprinkle the seeds thinly over the surface of the mix, cover with ¼ inch of potting mix, pat down, and water gently to avoid displacing the seeds. ¶ Place the pot outdoors where it will receive 4 to 6 hours of sun daily. Water consistently to keep the potting mix moist but not soggy, and fertilize every 2 weeks with a soluble organic fertilizer diluted to half strength.

Wildflowers
Miscellaneous species

What You Need
Seeds
Potting mix
All-purpose slow-release fertilizer granules
Container, 15 inches wide
by 12 inches deep
All-purpose soluble fertilizer

Growing Conditions
4 to 6 hours of sun each day

Hardiness
Tender; sow for summer only

When Flowers Bloom
Late spring to summer

POTTED
KITCHEN
GARDENS

In this day and age, when children think that beans grow on supermarket shelves and tomatoes spring from cans, growing your own vegetables in pots has a whiff of missionary duty about it. Still, whether you have a family needing tutoring in agriculture or remember the pleasure of the harvest from your own childhood, pots filled with fruits and vegetables can bring inestimable pleasure both to your kitchen and to your heart. Snipping a few herbs from pots on your balcony to sprinkle over a salad, or harvesting a bowl of cherry tomatoes for hors d'oeuvres can addict you to vegetable gardening in pots. ❧ A site with 4 to 6 hours of sunshine is necessary to grow warm-weather crops, although plants that grow in the cool of spring or fall, like lettuces and edible-pod peas, can do with a bit less sun.

Watch how the light changes in your growing area to make sure you have enough sun to spur on your plants, for too little light will result in spindly, weak growth with little harvest. A windy site makes a sunny deck cooler than one without breezes, and wind dries out potting mix quicker. ❧ Annuals like lettuce, squash, and tomatoes all want to grow quickly, with plenty of nutrients and consistent watering. Perennials like herbs or small shrubs like lemon verbena need a bit less attention as their growth is slower. Fruit trees on a dwarf rootstock do well in larger containers, although repotting yearly can be a bit of a chore. With large pots, you can apply a top dressing, pulling out as much of the potting mix as you can scrape off. Then reapply mix tossed with slow-release fertilizer granules. ❧ Make sure to match the varieties of plants to your climate. Tomatoes come in early, mid-season, and late varieties, based on the estimated number of days it will take the plant to go from seed to harvest. If you are short on room, consider vegetable types that have been hybridized to grow compactly in containers. Bush beans, squash, and determinate tomatoes (a bush type) often succeed better than their extravagantly long-limbed relatives, which take up space and need containers often too large for the tight spaces of most potted gardens. ❧ Only a few of the many possible potted edible gardens are mentioned here, so experiment with the whole range of delicious edibles you can grow in pots for your very own kitchen garden.

TOWER OF HARICOTS VERTS

The French term haricots verts *simply means "green beans," but these beans—oh what flavor and texture. As the French would emphasize, "Quelle différence!" Until you taste them, you might accuse the greengrocer of selling the skinniest, tiniest rejects. Called "French filet beans" in catalogues, they grow like plump toothpicks, and for maximum flavor and tenderness should be picked before they are 5 inches long. Originally, this was necessary because as they matured, the beans developed a tough string. Today, green* beans are stringless, but they should still be picked while young, tender, and succulent. ¶ *Haricots verts come in two growing types, both suited to containers. The bush varieties grow up to 2 feet tall, bloom, and produce beans over a limited time. To keep the chef happy, sow a new container of beans every week for a long harvest. Pole beans grow like vines, so they need a tall tripod to clamber up. They bloom all along the vines, so their period of harvest is naturally longer, but you will also have fewer beans ripening at any time. For a good long harvest, plant at least 2 large pots with 6 plants each. ¶ Sauté the beans briefly in olive oil and garlic, then toss them with salt and pepper. Make sure you don't eat them all right out of the pan.*

¶ HOW TO DO IT ¶ Plant your haricot vert seeds after the last chance of frost has passed. Soak the beans in water for up to 12 hours before planting. Measure the quantity of potting mix to almost fill the pot and add the correct amount of slow-release fertilizer granules according to the manufacturer's instructions. Moisten the mix thoroughly, tossing it to evenly distribute the granules. Add mix to the pot to fill it to 1 inch below the rim. If planting pole beans, insert 3 evenly spaced stakes around the edge of the pot, tying them at the top to make a tripod. Plant 6 seeds in the pot, ✧

Haricots Verts,
'Triumph de Farcy', 'Emerite'
Phaseolus vulgaris

ॐ

What You Need
Haricot vert seeds
Potting mix
All-purpose slow-release fertilizer granules
Container, 24 inches wide
and 20 inches deep
3 stakes to make a tripod for pole beans
All-purpose soluble organic fertilizer

ॐ

Growing Conditions
4 to 6 hours of sun each day

ॐ

Hardiness
Tender; sow for summer only

ॐ

When to Harvest
When beans are 4 to 5 inches long

ॐ

2 between each tripod stake. For bush beans, plant 3 evenly placed seeds around the edge of the pot. With your finger or a pencil, make a hole 1 inch deep for each bean. Drop in a bean, cover it with mix, and tamp the mix down. Water gently to avoid displacing the seeds. ¶ Place the pot outdoors where it will receive 4 to 6 hours of sun daily. Water consistently to keep the potting mix moist but not soggy, and fertilize every 2 weeks with a soluble organic fertilizer diluted to half strength. Harvest the beans when they are 4 to 5 inches long.

Mesclun salad bowl

Fresh salad greens add zip to any meal. Seed packets, generally called mesclun mix, offer a variety of different types of lettuces and greens chosen to grow together. A European tradition, these seed collections make harvesting a salad with as many as 7 or 8 different greens a matter of minutes when grown in a pot close to the kitchen door. Use the technique called "cut and come again" for multiple harvests from a single pot. When the leaves are about 3 or 4 inches long, cut them with scissors or a sharp knife to about ¹/₂ inch above the ground. When the whole container has been cut once, fertilize it and let the plants grow back to be harvested again. Using this technique, you can reap three or four harvests. By keeping a couple of pots growing, you can alternate between them, cutting from one pot while the other grows back. ¶ Mixes have been formulated for greens that grow well in the cool of spring or fall and are not prey to frosts after they have grown up, as well as for summer greens that can cope with high temperatures. Most seed companies clearly mark the different seasonal greens in the title, so, for the best results, make sure to match the right type to the season. In hot weather, place the salad pots in part shade and make sure to keep the mix constantly moist. ¶ **HOW TO DO IT** ¶ In the spring, plant your mesclun seeds after the last chance of frost has passed. Use these same cool-season seeds in the fall, starting them at the end of your summer season. Start summer seeds at the end of spring. Measure the quantity of potting mix to almost fill the pot and add the correct amount of slow-release fertilizer granules according to the manufacturer's instructions. Moisten the mix thoroughly, tossing it to evenly distribute the granules. Add mix to the pot to fill it to 1 inch below the rim. Sprinkle the seeds thinly over the surface of the mix, cover with ✐

Mesclun Salad Mix
Miscellaneous Species
❧

What You Need
Mesclun seeds
Potting mix
All-purpose slow-release fertilizer granules
Container, 24 inches wide
and 20 inches deep
All-purpose soluble organic fertilizer
❧

Growing Conditions
4 to 6 hours of sun each day
❧

Hardiness
Some mixes frost hardy,
some to sow for summer only
❧

When to Harvest
When leaves are 3 to 4 inches long
❧

¹/₄ inch of potting mix, pat down, and water gently to avoid displacing the seeds. ¶ Place the pot outdoors where it will receive 4 to 6 hours of sun daily. Water consistently to keep the potting mix moist but not soggy, and fertilize every 2 weeks with a soluble organic fertilizer diluted to half strength. Harvest when the leaves are 3 to 4 inches long.

LOTS OF THYME

Growing thyme links the gardener with a medicinal and culinary tradition that stretches back over centuries. *Native to the Mediterranean, thyme traveled throughout Europe with different conquerors, finding room in monastic herb gardens as a treatment for everything from melancholy and nightmares (a sachet under the pillow) to gout and bladder ailments (infusions). Thyme holds an honored place in the kitchen as well, as one of the preeminent herbs in European cuisines. From soup to fig jam, thyme, in its many different varieties, adds subtle flavor to foods.* ¶ *Use a wide, shallow container, for the small root balls do not need a pot with depth. Look for T. aureus, a golden-colored thyme, T. citriodorus, a strong lemon-scented type, and T. vulgaris, the common type most often used in cooking. A variegated type, called silver thyme, or T x citriodorus, is widely available and makes a handsome addition to a pot. If you like, plant each type in a separate pot.* ¶ **HOW TO DO IT** ¶ After the last chance of frost, pot up your thyme plants. Before planting, submerge the plants in their containers in a deep sink or bucket of water until the air ceases to bubble out of the containers. Measure the quantity of potting mix to almost fill the pot and add the appropriate amount of slow-release fertilizer granules according to the manufacturer's instructions. Moisten the mix thoroughly, tossing it to ensure an even distribution of the granules. Add enough mix to the pot to fill it to 2 inches below the rim. Scoop out enough mix to make a planting hole for each plant, spacing the holes 4 inches apart. Slide each plant out of its container and position the root ball in the middle of a planting hole. Add mix around the sides, tamping down as you go, continuing to add mix until it reaches the top of the root balls. Water again thoroughly, and add more mix if the sides slump below the level of any of the root balls. ¶ Place the container outdoors ✒

Thyme
Thymus species

❧

What You Need
4 assorted thyme plants in 4-inch pots
Potting mix
All-purpose slow-release fertilizer granules
Container, 15 inches wide by 6 inches deep
All-purpose soluble organic fertilizer

❧

Growing Conditions
4 to 6 hours of sun

❧

Hardiness
Tender

❧

When Blooms Appear
Spring to summer

❧

in a shady place to allow the plants to recover, watering it daily for 3 to 5 days, before placing it in its permanent site. Water consistently to keep the potting mix moist but not soggy, and fertilize every 2 weeks with a soluble organic fertilizer diluted to half strength. In fall, move the plant to an area that receives 4 to 6 hours of sunlight and is protected from below-freezing temperatures.

RECIPES

FOR POTTED

GARDENS

Taking the time to make your own, in this day and age—when the minutes seems to tick away faster than any metronome's setting—may seem like a waste of time and effort. Yet starting a project from scratch and enjoying it from beginning to end brings intense satisfaction. ❧ More and more often today, people turn to creative projects as respite from an all-too-busy lifestyle and an overwhelming stream of manufactured material goods. Just as some people love to make their own bread at home, despite the mountains of packaged and boutique loaves for sale, many gardeners prefer to make their own potting mixes despite the availability of commercial mixes. Making up quantities of your own mix in large batches allows you to control both the economics and the quality of the mix, including the amount and ratio of fertilizer you add. Storing the mixes in large garbage cans in your potting area allows you to easily pot up divisions or make cuttings, as well as to repot plants or pot up new purchases. Having a quick-draining or moisture-retaining mix on hand lets you suit the needs of your particular plants. If you specialize in plants requiring acid-based mixes, you can make adjustments to keep your plants well nourished. ❧ Similarly, although glazed terra-cotta pots abound, painting your own is not only fun, it allows you to design containers for an endless variety of effects. You can match your house tones, coordinate with blossom color, create a garden focal point, or install a blast of brilliance against a monochrome hedge. Even if you simply color a tiny pot as a gift for a friend, and plant it with a bulb of the same color, you will find your projects bring endless fascination and the joy of creative gardening.

THE POTTING SHED

Although a potting shed has a romantic flair, this utilitarian space makes the job of creating and maintaining pots a pleasure when all the necessary tools and equipment for potting up plants are right at hand. The space doesn't have to be the rustic shed smothered with flowering vines pictured in many magazines and books. It can be just a corner of a balcony, a couple of shelves in the garage, or a table set up on a deck with baskets or wooden boxes underneath to store useful items. ¶ First of all come the pots, as many of them as you can afford, in different sizes for maximum flexibility. Stack them so you can see what sizes you have available when potting up plants. Search out pots in garage sales and junkyards, and look for unusual containers such as colorful metal olive oil cans, brightly colored coffeepots, and even old boots. Even plastic buckets in neon colors can become containers after you punch holes in the bottom for drainage. ¶ Several metal storage cans, with lids or not, are useful to hold the ingredients for potting mixes as well as their finished combinations. If you are purchasing potting mix in plastic sacks, the sacks can be neatly stacked. Use commercial mixes or make your own specific to the types of plants you grow. Soil sieves, also called riddles, can be used to provide just the right texture for your mixes. ¶ A large shallow container or plastic bucket is useful for mixing fertilizer granule into potting mix. The shallow container or a sided tray or baking sheet is a good surface to use for filling pots as it helps to minimize cleanup. ¶ For growing seeds, you will want seedling containers, whether used six packs or Styrofoam trays providing growing slots for 30 or more seedlings. A special heating mat to place under the growing trays will make germination quicker and more successful. ¶ A number of tools are useful when working with containers. A dandelion weeder has a small head that can dig into a container and skillfully remove a weed or transplant. Small, narrow-headed trowels are designed to carry seedlings easily. A regular trowel can be used to set in bedding plants. A large serving spoon has a number of uses, including stirring ✦

What You Need
Assorted terra-cotta pots, metal tins,
flea market finds, other containers
Potting mixes, appropriate to your plants,
from moisture-loving ferns to dry cactus
Soil sieves
Tools such as a dandelion weeder,
seedling trowel, trowel,
serving spoon, turkey baster
Pruning tools such as clippers,
and racheting pruners
Watering cans
Hoses
✿

potting mix, filling pots, and scooping out holes to set in plants. ¶ Pruning shears are essential, both for trimming the top of the plants and the roots. Racheting pruners give extra strength to hands that may struggle to cut larger branches. ¶ Watering tools are essential. Watering cans come with a sprinkling head, poetically called a rose, that lets water softly trickle over newly seeded pots without displacing the seeds or breaking fragile seedlings down. Watering wands, which are sprinkling heads attached to long metal tubes, make it easy to direct water to specific locations when fastened to hoses. A turkey baster comes in handy when saucers underneath heavy pots are full to overflowing. They easily suck out the water to avoid staining wooden surfaces.

MAKING YOUR OWN POTTING SOIL

Mixes must be tailored to the water needs of specific plants. Plants like cactuses and succulents need to drain quickly, allowing the roots to dry out in between waterings. Ferns and begonias need a mix that holds water, to keep their roots continually moist. Plants like azaleas and rhododendrons need additional acid in their mix in order to thrive, while seeds do best in a fine-textured mix. ¶ You can use your own garden soil to make a potting mix, but make sure it does not have a history of soil-borne diseases such as verticillium wilt. (See page 22 for information on sterilizing your soil.) Adding builder's sand or perlite changes the composition of soil to allow better drainage for container plants. Peat moss increases the soil's capacity to hold water. ¶ Alternatively, you can purchase sterilized soil or put together a mix from inert materials to avoid the problems of disease. Seeds do well in a sterile mix, for seedings are particularly susceptible to fungus diseases. As seeds emerge, the first set of rudimentary leaves will not have the actual shape of the plant's leaves, but the second set, called the true leaves, will. Until seedlings get their first true leaves, they don't need any fertilizing, but as soon as growth gets underway, they use up large quantities of nutriments. ¶ Blending the ingredients takes very little time. Garbage cans make excellent storage containers. If you are using garden soil or have made homemade compost you will need to sift it first for a consistent texture. Garden stores or nurseries sell garden soil sifters with coarse-, medium- or fine-grade openings, depending upon the consistency you are striving for. You can easily make your own by stapling screening wire over a wooden square. If you make the square large enough to cover the top of a garbage can, it is easy to sift directly into the can. ¶ **HOW TO DO IT** ¶ If using sterilized garden soil or homemade compost, use a soil sifter to sort out pebbles, large bits of sticks, or bark. Measure out the proportions carefully. Add each ingredient and blend well.

Standard Potting Mix
ع

What You Need

2 parts screened garden soil

1 part peat moss or screened compost

1 part builder's sand, perlite, or vermiculite

Cactus/Succulent Potting Mix
ع

What You Need

1 part screened garden soil

1/2 part peat moss or screened compost

2 parts builder's sand, perlite, or vermiculite

Soil-less Mix
ع

What You Need

3 parts peat moss or screened compost

1 part builder's sand, perlite, or vermiculite

ع

PAINTED POTS

Painting your own pots allows you to match your decor, create a color scheme that coordinates with your flowers, and make personal gifts for family and friends. Even the artistically challenged can turn out charming pots with dots, informal stripes, or simple marbled surfaces. Embellishments like rubbed raised designs or gold or silver trim can transform a terra-cotta pot into an elegant and handsome container that suits a formal decor. Like a glaze, latex paint seals the pores of a clay pot for better water retention. Each pot takes about 4 days to complete, because you need to first seal it, then apply two coats of paint, then seal it again with a water-protecting clear coat, allowing the paint to dry thoroughly each time. Yet it takes such a short amount of time to paint each pot that you can work on a number of pots in different stages at the same time. ¶ **HOW TO DO IT** ¶ Use newly purchased pots or scrub up old pots to remove any dirt, moss or algae, or salts on the inside or outside surfaces. To seal the pots and make a smooth layer for the paint, brush the clean pots with masonry or terra-cotta sealer. Apply it carefully to avoid bubbles, as they will dry and create speckles on the surface when the pots are painted. After 24 hours, when the seal is thoroughly dry, add the first coat of latex paint. After 4 hours, or when that layer has dried thoroughly, add your second coat. Let that coat dry for 1 day, then paint or spray on the plastic sealer. ¶ Use foam brushes to paint broad stripes. Look for stencil brushes used in applying stencils—they are round daubers—to paint charmingly wobbly circles. Small bits of natural sponges dunked into paint and applied on top of a contrasting color create a spatter-ware look. Paint a light-colored top coat over a darker color, and let the bottom coat show through by rubbing off some of the top coat while it is still wet. Craft stores have gold, silver, or bronze rub, and applying it lightly to raised surfaces creates a burnished look.

Painted Pots

✿

What You Need

Terra-cotta pots

Masonry seal or terra-cotta seal

Small brushes

Latex paint

Varathane plastic sealer, available as spray or paint

✿

Resources

SEED AND PLANT SOURCES

Daffodil Mart
7463 Heath Trail
Gloucester, VA 23061
800 ALL-BULB
Excellent source of reliable and fine-quality bulbs.

Nichols Garden Nursery
1190 North Pacific Highway
Albany, OR 97321-45948
503 928-9280
Many different herbs.

Peaceful Valley Farm Supply
P.O. Box 2209
Grass Valley, CA 95945
916 272-4769
Natural pest management and organic fertilizers.

Ronniger's Seed Potatoes
Star Route
Moyie Springs, Idaho 83845
No phone, written orders only
Every potato you could want to plant.

Santa Barbara Heirloom
Seedling Nursery
P.O. Box 4235
Santa Barbara, CA 93140
805 968-5444
Ships vegetable seedlings.

Seeds Blum
HC Idaho City Stage
Boise, ID 83706
800 528-3658
Excellent seeds for vegetables and flowers.

Shepherd's Garden Seeds
30 Irene Street
Torrington, CN 06790
203 482-3638
Good mesclun collections.

Vermont Bean Seed Company
Garden Lane
Fair Haven, VT 05743
803 663-0217
Filet beans, among other vegetables.

Bibliography

Bailey, L. H.
The Standard Cyclopedia of Horticulture.
New York: Macmillan, 1950.

Hobhouse, Penelope.
Penelope Hobhouse's Gardening Through the Ages.
New York: Simon & Schuster, 1992.

Hortus Third Dictionary.
New York: Macmillan, 1976.

Jellicoe, Geoffrey and Susan; Goode,
Patrick; and Lancaster, Michael.
Oxford Companion to Gardens.
New York: Oxford University Press, 1991.

Kourik, Robert.
*Designing and Maintaining Your Edible
Landscape Naturally.*
Santa Rosa: Metamorphic Press, 1986.

Sunset Western Garden Book.
Menlo Park: Sunset Publishing
Corporation, 1995.

INDEX

ACKNOWLEDGMENTS

Like a collection of potted plants, this book gained inspiration, assistance, and form from many different sources. At the Lescher Agency, Susan Lescher, Mickey Choate, and Carolyn Larson began the process, like selecting the best pots. At Chronicle Books, Leslie Jonath and Carole Goodman oversaw the schedule, the basis of it all, just as the best potting soil sustains plants. Carolyn Miller's elegant copyediting weeded out errors and nourished the prose. The careful design of Aufuldish & Warinner brought a sense of vision and order to the whole. Susan Carr; Calloways Nursery in Santa Rosa, California; Robert Kourik; Fredrique Lavoipierre of Shoestring Nursery in Sebastapol, California; Anne Leyhe; and Hazel White provided inspiration, as water for plants feeds their thirst. Faith's inspirators included Beth and John, James and Gary, Joan and Jim, Tor and Susan, Flim and Lisa, Kathy, Trisha, Pat, Ruthie, Cree, Alta, and her friends at Tantau in St. Helena, California. And, like a trellis that plants clamber up, Mimi and Faith were blessed with the support of Bruce and Arann and Daniel Harris.